RERA SIMPLIFIED

Amaanuddin Siddique
Adv. Darsh Dharod
Dr. Adv. Harshul Savla

INDIA · SINGAPORE · MALAYSIA

ISBN
Paperback 979-8-89673-378-2
Hardcase 979-8-89673-779-7

Contents

About the Author

Amaan Siddique is a 20-year-old student with a profound interest in real estate. He achieved remarkable academic success at Beacon High School, Mumbai, where he served as head boy, scoring 99% in his ICSE examinations and 96% in his ISC examinations at Jasudben ML School. Currently, he is pursuing a degree in Statistics and Economics at St. Xavier's College, Mumbai, which is recognized as the number one autonomous college in India. This prestigious institution is renowned for its rigorous academic standards, holistic education approach, and strong emphasis on research and extracurricular activities.

Amaan's passion for the real estate industry stems from his early exposure to it through his father, Moinuddin Siddique, who is the founder of Doors Realty, a company renowned for its consultation in luxury real estate in Mumbai. He has also gained valuable insights from his maternal uncle, Naveen Nandwani, Managing Director at Savills. Working alongside his father has provided Amaan with invaluable experiences, deepening his love for the industry. He wishes to work in real estate moving forward and hopes to bring about positive changes by leveraging his diverse academic knowledge and industry experience. He has also had the privilege of learning from esteemed professionals such as Dr. Adv. Harshul Savla, which has further deepened his appreciation for the field.

In addition to his academic and professional pursuits, Amaan is an active social advocate, involved with NGOs that focus on environmental conservation. He has participated in significant initiatives, including protests to protect Aarey Forest. Amaan also has a keen interest in sports and fitness, having played cricket at a professional level, and he is dedicated to maintaining a healthy lifestyle. In his leisure time, he enjoys wildlife photography, capturing the beauty of nature.

About the Author

Adv. Darsh Rekha Ketan Dharod is a young millennial of 27 years having keen interest and plethora of knowledge about the Real Estate Industry.

Adv. Darsh has been keenly watching and tracking the real estate industry from about when he was in his pre-teens, the spark and interest kicked-off in him while visiting a few under construction projects and subsequent interactions with key stakeholders and stalwarts from the industry.

Adv. Darsh is an alumnus of Bombay Scottish School, Mahim an institution which is 176 years old, ranked among the top 2 in Mumbai and top 6 in India. He stood among the top 1 percent in the ICSE Board 10th Grade examinations.

Adv. Darsh has degrees in Accountancy, Finance, Management and Law having studied Bachelors of Accountancy and Finance (B.A.F) from H.R. College of Commerce and Economics in which he stood at 6th Rank in entire University of Mumbai, Bachelors of Law (LL.B) from K.C. Law College, Masters of Commerce in Management (M.Com) and Masters of Law (LL.M) from University of Mumbai and is currently in the last and final stage of completing Chartered Accountancy (CA) from Institute of Chartered Accountants of India and Chartered Financial Analyst (CFA) from CFA Institute, USA.

Adv. Darsh started working rather at an early age of 19 years while still in college, managing both studies and work which has helped him work in different industries.

Adv. Darsh as part of Chartered Accountancy course has completed 3 years of articleship, there after worked in Tata Capital, a Tata Group Company in Special Projects developing a new digitally enabled platform driving collaboration among its business enabling the dream of 'One Tata' which eventually took the shape as the super app 'Tata Neu'.

He later worked at HDFC Property Ventures a Real Estate Private Equity Fund and a HDFC Group Company and IEG Investment Banking Group, a German based Investment Bank. He has also worked at Colliers International in their Consulting and Advisory team, in which he advised on various Real Estate Developments and Asset classes to top Developers, Industrialists and Governments in 25 cities across 7 States and 2 UTs in India.

In his stint at Adani Realty, in CEOs Office- Strategic Projects, he was part of the founding member team for Dharavi Redevelopment Project which is Asia's Largest Slum Rehabilitation and Urban Regeneration Project. Currently, in Godrej Properties, he is a part of the Business Development, Investments and Acquisition team, responsible for acquiring new greenfield and brownfield projects for Godrej Properties in form of Land acquisitions, Strategic Investments and Redevelopment opportunities.

Adv. Darsh has been recipient of many prestigious awards in his life such as the "R.K. Sharma Memorial Prize" for highest distinction in ICSE Examinations, Letter of Appreciation from Mr. Rajendra Darda, Editor-in-chief Lokmat and Minister of School Education in Government of Maharashtra. He was felicitated with various awards during his college years for his contribution to college and academic performance by Dr. Indu Shahani, Principal of H.R. College of Commerce and Economics and former Sheriff of Mumbai. He's also been recipient of awards by Bombay Scottish School, K.C. Law College, KVO, LNMA among many others.

Adv. Darsh is actively involved and one of the youngest committee members in the history of CREDAI MCHI (Confederation of Real Estate Developers' Association of India & Maharashtra Chamber of Housing Industry), where he is a part of Statistics and Research Wing. CREDAI MCHI has more than 1800 Developers as its members across 14 City Chapters making up for entire Mumbai Metropolitan Region.

Adv. Darsh is also actively involved and is also one of the youngest committee members in the history of CREDAI National Youth Wing, where he is a part of Business Process Automation Committee. CREDAI National has more than 13,300 Developers as its members in 21 States and 230 City Chapters across India.

Adv. Darsh is also an International Best Selling Author and has authored more than a dozen books on the Real Estate Sector, making his books one of India's and perhaps the World's most comprehensive literatures on Real Estate Sector. Some of his books are: Self-Redevelopment & Reviving Stalled Projects, Alternative Real Estate, Insolvency & Bankruptcy Code, Judicial Journey under RERA, ERA post RERA, Funding Options for Developers, FSI- A Development Control Tool, The Redevelopment Guide, etc. The books are available in countries such as but not limited to Singapore, Australia, UK, Canada, Japan, UAE, Germany among many others. The books are available on online portals such as Amazon, Flipkart, Rakuten Kobo, Apple iBooks, Google Play Books, Amazon Kindle, Notion Press across several countries.

Adv. Darsh due to his rich and diversified academic and professional experience, regularly holds Seminars and is also a Guest Lecturer on different topics covering Finance, Law, Real Estate, among others at prestigious colleges in India. He has also written articles and snippets for a few newspapers, magazines and journals.

Adv. Darsh has mentored over 50 students pursuing their Masters, MBA and other specialization courses from institutions and universities such as NMIMS, IIT- Kharagpur, CEPT, NICMAR, RICS, GLC, MIT, UC Berkley, Cranfield, HSNC, Nirma, KC law, Amity among others. Adv. Darsh has also been the guide for final year Dissertation, Thesis, DRP for many of the above students.

Adv. Darsh is also a podcaster, and has hosted and interviewed few of the top experts from the Real Estate Industry through the podcasts, specifically, he has been a host in the Podcast series "The Deep Dive" by CREDAI National which is available across mediums such as Youtube and Spotify, focussing on deep diving into some key aspects related to the real estate industry in India

Adv. Darsh is also actively involved in a few NGOs and for his contributions to society has been facilitated by Ministry of Railways, Government of India among many other organizations. He has also represented India at an UNESCO event held in Europe and Turkey.

Adv. Darsh has keen interest in sports, has run several marathons and been a gold medalist in Swimming, Chess and Badminton.

About the Author

Dr. Adv. Harshul Savla (MRICS) is Managing Partner of M Realty (Suvidha Lifespaces) which has successfully completed more than 2 million sq.ft. in last 35 years across Mumbai City under the able leadership of Mr. Pramesh Rambhiya. CRISIL India and Realty Icon Awards recognized Dr. Harshul as "Young Thought Leader" and Realty NXT featured him as "Young Turk of Real Estate Sector". He has won the prestigious CREDAI-MCHI Golden Pillar Award in the category of Best Debutant Real Estate Developer and has been awarded "Young Achiever of the Year" by ET NOW, CNN News 18, ZEE Business, MAHARASHTRA Times, ABP News, Realty+, MID DAY, Business World and Realty Quarter.

Dr. Harshul has featured in the Business World and Realty Plus "40 under 40" list as Real Estate's Young Turk consecutively in 2021, 2022, 2023 and 2024. He has also been awarded the prestigious "Pillars of Maharashtra" award in 2022 by Hon'ble Member of Parliament for Mumbai North. The Times Group's Economic Times has awarded Dr. Harshul Savla as an Inspiring Personality 2022 for exceptional contribution to Real Estate Sector. Mid Day's "Success Stories 2022" has featured Dr. Harshul's various achievements and journey. He has been a TEDx Speaker too.

Dr. Harshul has worked as EA to Ramesh Nair, former Chairman, JLL India and has worked in the Wealth Management Team at TATA Capital where he was awarded the National Award for Exemplary Performance. He is a perfect blend of Corporate Experience along with stellar education credentials of Ph.D., LL.M, LL.B, MBA and BMS from prestigious institutions like JBIMS, GLC, NM and Department of Law, University of Mumbai.

Dr. Harshul holds the World Record for "Maximum Degree from Single University" and his World Record is mentioned in World Book of Records London, The British World Records, International Book of Records, International Talent Book of Records, Exclusive World Record, Asian World Records, Global Records & Research Foundation, Amazing Indian Records, World Records India, India Book of Records, Kohinoor Vidyasamrat, Champion Book of World Record, High Range Book of World Records etc.

He also holds the World Record for "Maximum Books Authored & Published in a Year" for authoring and publishing 12 Real Estate Books in the year 2021 in English Language. Dr. Harshul is awarded as "Author of the Year" at the prestigious CNBC Awaaz Real Estate Excellence Awards 2022 held at Taj Lands End, Mumbai.

Dr. Harshul was awarded Doctorate (Ph.D.) for his Thesis on REITs (Real Estate Investment Trusts) which is first such thesis in India on the said subject and the Thesis is also available in the form of a book. Apart from this he is an NSE Certified Market Professional - Level 4 and has done a course on 'Strategic Real Estate Management' from ISB, Hyderabad.

Dr. Harshul is "Chairman: Statistics & Standards" at CREDAI National, which has more than 13,300 Real Estate Developers as its Members and has presence in 230 Cities (21 State Chapters). He is Research Convenor of CREDAI MCHI and heads its Statistics & Research Wing. CREDAI MCHI is a leading Real Estate Developers Association of MMR having 1,800 members across its 14 Units. Dr. Harshul has also served as the National Head of the Committee on E-Learning and Masterclass at CREDAI National Youth Wing from 2021-2023 and is presently the "Chairman: Business Process Optimization"

Dr. Harshul is also an Amazon Best Selling Author and has authored 22 books on the Real Estate Sector and General Management, making his books one of India's most comprehensive literatures on Real Estate Sector. Some of his books are: Real Estate Laws, Reality of Realty, Real Estate Valuation, Affordable Housing, NBFC & HFC Crisis, Fractional Ownership & REITs, Insolvency & Bankruptcy Code, Self-Redevelopment & Reviving Stalled Projects, Digitalizing Real

Estate Sector in Built Environment, Building Information Modeling, Green Buildings, Facility Management, COVID-O-NOMICS, Luxury Retail, Alternative Real Estate, Judicial Journey under RERA, Self-Redevelopment and Reviving Stalled Projects, NCLT & IBC in Real Estate Sector, ERA POST RERA, Funding Options for Developers, FSI – A Development Control Tool, The Redevelopment Guide, MAHA RERA etc. He regularly writes articles for fortnightly business magazine "Property House" and may other newspapers and journals.

Dr. Harshul is Associate Professor at ITM University and is also a Ph.D. Guide / Supervisor with them. He was a Visiting Faculty and Guest Lecturer at the prestigious RICS School of Built Environment, Mumbai Campus. He taught the subject 'Real Estate Development Process' to Management Students at the Mumbai Campus. He was also a Guest Lecturer at REMI - The Real Estate Management Institute, Mumbai. He was Invited to conduct Session on REITs in India for Developers Members of NAREDCO and was one of the youngest Member Developer to do so. He has also delivered a lecture at PEATA (I) on Future of Realty. He is also a renowned moderator for panels discussing various aspects of Realty and has moderated more than 60 panel discussions so far.

Dr. Harshul has recently embarked his research journey for his second Ph.D. which he is pursuing from the Department of Law, University of Mumbai under the guidance of Former HOD of the Department. His thesis is on the topic of RERA and will be the first Ph.D. in Law thesis in India on RERA.

Dr. Harshul is also the Founding Member of the "RERA Practitioners' Welfare Association" and the Founding Member of "IRIYA Realty Intelligentsia and Advisory Foundation of India" which comprises of Innovation Centre, Think Tank and Centre of Excellence. Dr. Harshul is also part of the Managing Committee of IBG (India Business Group). Dr. Harshul is a Founding Member at the 500 MBA Club and also a Mentor at the Founder Institute which is the world's most proven network to turn ideas into fundable startups and startups into global businesses.

Part 1
Overview of RERA

Many central and state government laws overlook India's real estate sector, which, despite having multiple laws, remains largely unorganised and unregulated.

The real estate sector has come under tremendous pressure since 2015. Many real estate projects had been halted, and numerous builders had misused the funds of the homebuyers, who had invested their lifetime savings into purchasing the properties. They had limited recourse to rapidly resolving their problems. There were no regulations to aid the homebuyers and prevent promoters from cheating their customers. Homebuyers needed transparency, discipline, and the timely delivery of projects.

To address this issue, the government enacted a new legislation called the "Real Estate Regulation and Development Act of 2016," that came into effect on May 1, 2017, across India.

A few reasons for the enactment of RERA are the following: -

- Lack of transparency by Promoters
- Fraud and cheating by Builders
- Selling of open spaces and parking
- OC and CC were not provided
- Delaying the date of possession
- Flats sold at Super Built-up areas
- Lack of efficient redressal

And many more.

The Act applies to residential, commercial, plotted, and all types of business development and sale of real estate projects. The registration of real estate projects has been made compulsory in the planning area, where the size of land proposed to be developed is more than 500 sq. meters or where the number of apartments proposed to be developed is more than 8. The promoters must disclose all relevant information relating to the project and provide quarterly updates about the work progress. The promoter will not decide on any changes in the project without obtaining consent from 2/3rd allottees.

RERA requires all involved personnel, such as builders, developers, and real estate agents, to register under the Act.

Chapter 1

Objectives and Purpose of RERA

The prominent objective of RERA is to bring transparency, confidence, and trust to real estate buyers. RERA wishes to establish a real estate regulatory authority that regulates and promotes the sector. The Act protects buyers' interests and encourages the timely delivery of properties or projects. RERA was also enacted to boost investment in the industry.

The objectives of RERA are

- Establish a Regulatory Authority (RERA) to regulate and keep the real estate sector in check.
- To provide greater transparency and a grievance system for homebuyers in the real estate sector.
- To prevent the builders from misusing the buyers' funds.
- To impose a compulsion upon the promoter in any real estate project to register the project with the Authority.
- To review the authenticity of promoters, real estate projects, and agents.
- To protect the rights of the buyers.
- To make the allottees aware of their duties.
- To impose an obligation on the real estate agent not to facilitate the sale or purchase of any plot, apartment, or building without registering himself with the Authority.
- To curb unnecessary delays in the delivery of projects.
- To impose liability upon the promoter to pay compensation to the allottees provided under the legislation if he fails to discharge any obligations.
- To set up an Appellate System as a grievance redressal system.
- To establish the Real Estate Appellate Tribunal to handle appeals, ensure compliance, dispute resolution, issue orders and directions, enforce penalties, and oversee regulatory practices.

- To help bring confidence into the real estate sector.
- Establish an advisory to advise and recommend the central government on implementing the proposed legislation.
- The RERA Act is a leap towards transforming the real estate sector in India to encourage greater transparency, accountability, and financial discipline and finally instilling greater trust and confidence in the industry.

Chapter 2

Powers and Functions of RERA

1. The chairperson has powers of superintendence and directions in conducting the Authority's affairs and shall preside over all its meetings.
2. The Authority shall recommend changes to the appropriate government to facilitate the growth and promotion of a healthy, organized, transparent, and efficient Real Estate Sector.
3. Opinions on matters relating to real estate must be given to an appropriate government within 60 days of receipt of such request.
4. To keep the real estate sector regulated by looking after all registrations of promoters and agents to publish and maintain a records website.
5. To maintain a database on its website for public viewing.
6. To ensure compliance of all the involved parties.
7. Call for information and conduct any investigation in any matter it finds necessary.
8. To issue any interim orders.
9. To impose penalty or interest on any defaulter.
10. To rectify its orders within two years from the order date.

Part 2
Homebuyer's Corner

Chapter 1

Definitions by RERA

Title of a property

The title is a legal term; it means the ownership right to a property. The nature of a title can be the following: Leasehold, freehold, or development right. Everyone's prime concern at the time of purchasing a property is its title. Every property has a title, which is evidence of the right of ownership. It is a legal principle that a person is unable to convey a better title than what he already has. A clear title to a property is one of the most important factors to be considered before a purchase. Hence, the buyer should undertake due diligence to ascertain the existence, nature, and marketability of the title and the ability of the seller to convey a clear and marketable title free from encumbrance.

RERA would ask the Promoter to produce the following documents for review -

Government orders for grants, succession certificates, sale deeds, gift deeds, wills, partition deeds, etc., evidencing the transfer of title over the years.

If a seller claims development rights to a property, then the power of attorney and the development agreement executed by the owners in favor of the seller should be produced.

All title documents should be stamped and registered by the concerned official at the office of the jurisdictional sub-registrar of assurances. The Khata should be registered in the seller's name. All information regarding pending and past litigation should be known.

Sale Deed

An Original sale deed is a registered proof of transfer and sale of ownership of the property from the seller to the buyer. The original title deed in the seller's name should be checked to ensure the property is not mortgaged. It is vital that before the Sale Deed is executed, one should execute the sale agreement and check for compliance with the terms and conditions as agreed upon between the parties.

If a minor executes a sale deed, prior permission to sell must be obtained from the court for subsequent ratification. If a Power of Attorney holder executes the permission, then a copy of such Power of Attorney should be checked to verify its authenticity.

Allotment letter and possession letter

Suppose a property is acquired from the State Industrial Areas Development Board or another statutory Development authority. In that case, documents relating to the allotment, lease cum sale agreement, possession certificate, or builder-buyer agreement need to be checked.

Check the registrar's office to see if the builder has not mortgaged the property. Homebuyers must also know that the builder cannot mortgage the sold units. He only has rights to the unsold units within the project.

It is now mandatory to share mortgage details with the Central Registry of Securitization Asset Reconstruction and Security Interest of India (CERSAI). A buyer can now access this database and check if their property details show up against any loans issued.

https://www.cersai.org.in/CERSAI/home.prg

A homebuyer can also demand a No Objection Certificate (NOC) from the builder for the property. The NOC should be made on a 10 Rupee stamp paper and duly notarized. Lastly, the buyer can also issue a public notice stating that anyone can object to the property they intend to buy.

Further, as per the Real Estate (Regulation and Development) Act, 2016 (RERA) regulations, the builders must disclose the details pertinent to the property mortgage. These details will be part of the RERA certificate and benefit the buyer. If a property is mortgaged after receiving the documents, the builder must update these details in the quarterly or annual report submitted under RERA.

Mother Deed/Parent Deed

A property may have passed through various hands, resulting in different ownerships at different points in time. The buyer needs to know the origin of the property. A mother deed contains all the previous owners' details in chronological order. This involves checking all the 'chain of documents' for the last thirty years at least.

Land Records (7/12 extract or RTC)

7/12 extract is an extract in the land registers of districts in Maharashtra. In Marathi, it is called "Saath Baara Utara." These records are maintained by the Revenue Department of the Government of Maharashtra. They serve as proof of ownership of agricultural land, showing details such as occupancy, ownership, liabilities, rights, and other aspects pertaining to its ownership. Village Form VII and Village Form XII are combined to create the 7/12 extract.

These are the rights records: tenancy and cultivation issued by the Registrar of Land Holdings and obtained from the Tehsildar's office. The nomenclature of land records varies from state to state. Mutation is the transfer of title entry in revenue records of the local municipal corporation, containing details about the type of ownership, number of owners and their shares of the property, loan on the property, tenant in the property (if any), cultivable and non-cultivable areas in the property, source of irrigation (if any), assessment for the property. These extracts may not cover all the persons' names, so checking mutation entries is advisable.

The Maharashtra government launched the Bhulekh Mahabhumi Maharashtra Land Record initiative to provide the people of the state with important information relating to land records quickly and easily online through the website, without having to visit the office of the Tehsildar of the respective district.

https://bhulekh.mahabhu-mi.gov.in

Property Card

A property card is proof of land ownership and is of great importance as it serves its purpose in many different situations. It is required when buying or selling a plot of land and can be requested by a wide range of stakeholders, such as local government bodies, banks, property agents, etc. It can come in handy to settle any property disputes, prevent the illegal grabbing of land, and detect false claims of ownership by a party.

Khata extract and certificate

When a new registration is obtained after paying the tax, a Khata certificate is issued to the property owner or his family members. It states that a particular property No. "X" is in Mr. Y. This certificate is required to apply for a water connection, electricity connection, trade license, and building license.

Ceiling Limit

There is a limit provided for the holding of land according to the type of property. The buyer should check that the land he is purchasing does not exceed its limit. 8 An extract is a document that gives an idea about the exact holding of the owner; therefore, it is advisable to check the document to calculate the total holding of the present owner.

6C Certificate

The 6C Certificate is a document that gives us an idea about the names of all Legal Heirs of a deceased person. This document is of great importance as there are certain ambiguities in which the name of female legal heirs would not appear on revenue documents. To avoid this issue, it is advisable to check the 6C certificate.

Encumbrance certificates

It ensures that the property is free from any legal and monetary liabilities. An Encumbrance Certificate shows all the records of buying/selling or transactions and mortgaging. It gives the buyer all the details about the property transactions.

The certificates can be obtained at the sub-registrar office or the web portal of the Ministry of Corporate Affairs. Before completing the transaction, the purchaser may issue a public notice in the newspapers calling for claims from interested third parties, if any.

Maps

It is advisable to check maps provided by the government authorities; this will give you a better idea of the exact location and access to the property.

Status of Tax Payments

Non-payment of property taxes results in a charge on the property, thus affecting its marketability. For this reason, the buyer must verify with the municipal authorities whether the seller has defaulted on payment of property taxes.

The buyer must ask for all utility bill receipts from the seller. Once the property is transferred in the buyer's name, the buyer will be liable to pay all pending dues against the property, whether utility or otherwise.

One may investigate if there exists any ongoing proceedings against the seller u/s 281 of the Income-tax Act, 1961. Suppose the seller is a non-resident of India. In that case, TDS may be deductible from the consideration paid unless the concerned Income-tax officer obtains a certificate for non-deduction or lower deduction.

Conversion and land-use permissions

With increasing urbanization and merging revenue lands with urban conglomerates, the conversion of property for NA use is of crucial significance since a number of state law prevent the purchase of agricultural land by non-agriculturists.

Secondly, the homebuyer must examine the Master Plan and check if the property is developed according to the zoning plan—such as residential, commercial, industrial, public/semi-public, parks and open spaces, etc. If the actual use differs from what the Town planning committte permits, prior permission is required.

Construction Approvals

Before purchasing a property, the buyer must check the construction approvals of the land to ensure that it is clear of all complications.

The buyer must also inquire about CRZ and other zones, as development in such zones is prohibited. No deed should be signed unless the inquiry is made.

Commencement certificate (for under-construction property)

A Commencement certificate is one such legal document that is issued by the local authorities after inspecting a site. Non-availability of a Commencement Certificate will result in the construction being considered illegal, levying penalties, and can even attract an eviction notice.

Completion certificate (for a constructed property)

The municipal authorities issue a completion certificate denoting that the building complies with the rules relating to height, distance from the road, construction according to the approved plans, etc.

NOC from the Electricity Department/Pollution Control Board/ Water Works/Airport Authority

To ensure government approvals are in place, a no-objection certificate from all government departments and an NOC from the revenue authority for the property sale are also required.

Chapter 2

Due Diligence for Purchasing a Property

Why is it necessary?

Conducting due diligence by a homebuyer before buying a flat is essential for ensuring a secure and informed investment. This process involves verifying the property's legal compliance by checking titles, obtaining clearances from municipal and environmental authorities, and confirming that the property is free from legal disputes and unpaid dues. Ensuring the builder's credentials, financial stability, and registration under Maha RERA is crucial for transparency and accountability. Proper due diligence also helps detect fraudulent practices, multiple sales of the same property or falsified documents. Evaluating the construction quality and availability of promised amenities ensures you get value for your money.

Additionally, understanding market trends, potential developments, and the property's proximity to essential services helps assess its resale and rental value. Aligning with bank loan eligibility requirements and confirming no pending liabilities such as taxes or utility bills further safeguard your financial interests. This investigation minimizes risks, ensures legal and economic protection, and supports a well-informed purchasing decision.

Due Diligence

1. The allottees should understand the implications of (a) forfeiture clause wordings/liquidated damages wordings and (b) force majeure clauses. They should ensure the reduction of forfeiture money to a minimum or incorporate no forfeiture of the agreement upon force majeure situations, such as permanent incapacity or death of the allottee.
2. The allottees should ensure that no direct or indirect price escalation clauses are embedded in the agreement for sale. Price

escalation is not allowed under MOFA and RERA, and the allottees should insist on deleting such clauses.

3. The allottees should check the encumbrances, pending cases, disputes, promoter's reputation, financial strength, and integrity before booking.
4. The allottees should book only when fully satisfied with the promoters, the project, and its completion.
5. The allottees should ensure that the possession date is clearly defined and not loosely worded with grace periods in the body, further grace periods in schedules and annexures, or diluted with words like "extendable due to lack of permission from authorities." They should be alert to inconsistencies regarding the completion date per the RERA web portal and dilutions in the sale agreement. The allottees can seek the promoter's incorporation of an earlier possession date if promised for their flat.
6. The allottees should seek the help of a professional to guide and advise before booking.
7. The allottees should verify the reputation of the promoter.
8. The allottees should thoroughly review the agreement for sale and allotment letter available on the Maha RERA website and satisfy themselves with all terms and conditions.
9. The new trend is to book in RTM (ready-to-move) projects consequent to OC, thereby eliminating most risks for the allottee.
10. Upon identifying a project of their choice, the allottees should check all the available documents about the project and promoters on the RERA website.
11. The allottees should ensure that the agreement for sale is similar to the model agreement under RERA and that it benefits them.
12. The allottees should discuss any deviations from the model agreement for sale prescribed under RERA with the promoter.
13. The allottees should understand their rights and duties and the promoter's duties, responsibilities, and obligations under the RERA Act and Rules.

A few of the documents a homebuyer should inspect before purchasing a property

1. Periodic status of construction level.
2. Joint Development Agreement (JDA) - check agreement terms and conditions.
3. Proforma of sale deed, sale agreement, allotment letter, conveyance deed.
4. Sanctioned plan from the appropriate Authority.
5. Affidavit filed by promoters.
6. Title insurance and other insurance details.
7. RERA Registration certificate and project details on the Maha RERA website.
8. Legal title report of the land.
9. Details of layout.
10. Details of professionals like Chartered Accountants, architects and engineers.
11. Specification of standard amenities and infrastructure, common areas.
12. Experience of promoters and the status of these projects.
13. Cost break-up of the unit to be purchased.
14. Specification of the unit to be purchased.
15. Sanctioned building plan.
16. FSI or TDR details.
17. Amount of government taxes and duties to be paid.
18. Brief details of the promoter company, names, and photos of promoters.
19. Details regarding architecture and design standards.
20. Parking charges, if any.
21. Location details of the project.

22. If a project loan is taken, then details of the loan and mortgage details.

Steps to carry out after purchasing a property

The allottees must keep checking the project's progress on the RERA website.

A homebuyer should follow these general steps -

1. Visit the RERA Website:

Go to the RERA website of the specific state where the project is located. Each state in India has its own RERA website, such as Maharashtra RERA (MahaRERA), Karnataka RERA (K-RERA), etc.

2. Search for the Project:

- Look for a section labelled "Project Status," "Project Details," or similar.
- Use the search function to find the project. You can typically search by the project name, RERA registration number, builder/ developer name, or location.

3. Access Project Details:

- Once you locate the project, click on its name or registration number to view detailed information.
- This section usually includes key details such as project registration date, expected completion date, and specifications.

4. Review Progress Reports:

- Check for links or tabs within the project details page labelled "Progress Reports," "Quarterly Updates," or similar.
- RERA mandates that builders update the project's progress quarterly. These reports typically include updates on construction status, financial disclosures, legal approvals, and more.

5. Examine the Updates:

- Download or view the latest progress reports for detailed updates on the project's status.

- Compare these updates with previous reports to gauge the overall progress and any delays or issues.

6. Check for Additional Documents:

- Look for other important documents such as sanctioned plans, layout plans, and certificates related to completion or occupancy.
- These documents provide further assurance about the project's compliance and progress.

7. Contact Information:

- If you have specific queries or need clarification, use the contact information provided for the developer or the RERA helpdesk.
- The RERA websites also offers grievance redressal where buyers can report issues or seek assistance.

A few tips for homebuyers while purchasing a property

- Regular Monitoring: Regularly check the RERA website for new updates, especially for projects under construction.
- Compare with Physical Site Visits: If possible, complement the online information with actual site visits to verify the reported progress.
- Legal Consultation: A homebuyer could consult with a legal expert for a detailed understanding and verification of the project's compliance status.

By following these steps, home buyers can effectively monitor their project's progress and ensure they are well-informed about its status and compliance with regulatory requirements.

After checking a project's progress report on the RERA website, a home buyer should take the following steps to ensure they remain informed and proactive about their investment:

1. Verify Physical Progress:

- Site Visits: Regularly visit the site to verify the progress reported on the RERA website personally.

- Photos and Videos: Take photographs or videos during your site visits to document the progress and compare them with the RERA updates.

2. **Stay in Touch with the Developer:**
   - Regular Communication: Regularly communicate with the developer or builder for direct updates and clarifications on the project's progress.
   - Attend Meetings: Participate in any meetings or discussions organized by the developer for home buyers.
3. **Engage with Other Buyers:**
   - Form a Group: Connect with other buyers through social media, forums, or WhatsApp groups to share information and experiences.
   - Collective Actions: Coordinate with other buyers for collective actions or representations to the developer or RERA if needed.
4. **Monitor Financial Transactions:**
   - Payment Schedule: Ensure your payments align with the construction milestones and the progress reported.
   - Receipts and Documentation: Keep all receipts, agreements, and communication documented for future reference.
5. **Review Legal Compliance:**
   - Legal Consultation: Consult a real estate lawyer to review the project's legal compliance and the terms of your agreement with the developer.
   - Documentation Verification: Ensure all required legal documents, such as approved plans and NOCs, are in order.
6. **Address Grievances:**
   - Lodge Complaints: If you notice discrepancies or delays in the project, lodge a formal complaint on the RERA website.
   - Follow-up: Follow up on any complaints or grievances filed to ensure they are addressed.

7. **Plan for Possession:**

   - Final Inspection: A thorough inspection of the property prior to taking possession it matches the desired standards.
   - Occupancy Certificate: Verify that the developer has obtained the occupancy certificate before you move in.

8. **Stay Updated on RERA Notices:**

   - Regular Checks: Regularly check the RERA website for any new notices, orders, or updates related to the project.
   - Subscribe to Updates: If available, subscribe to notifications or newsletters from the RERA website for automatic updates.

Benefits to Allottees under RERA

Application for registration of real estate project documents and details available to allottees on the RERA webpage of the project.

The documents available on the website are

- Enterprise details
- Project details
- Copies of approvals and commencement certificate
- Sanctioned plan, layout plan, and project specifications
- Plan of development works of the projects and facilities
- Location details, demarcation of land, its boundaries, latitude and longitude of the project endpoints
- Proformas of allotment letter, sale agreement, and conveyance deed.
- Number, type, and carpet area of apartments
- Areas of exclusive balconies or verandas and open terrace area
- Number and area of garages
- Real estate agents
- Contractors, architects, structural engineers, and other persons concerned with project development
- The promoter's declaration-cum-affidavit in Form B contains the legal title and valid title documents, encumbrances, period for

project completion, escrow account deposits and withdrawals, on-time pending approvals, and furnishing documents prescribed by rules and regulations.

Past track record of the promoter

At the time of registration, the Promoters shall provide details of the projects completed by them in the last five years, as well as the promised date of possession and the actual date of possession. The promoters should also provide all the details about the proposed and approved FSI.

Revocation of Registration u/s 7

The allottees may file a complaint before the Authority for revocation of registration to protect their interests if a promoter defaults in any respect of the provisions of the Act or the Rules or regulations made thereunder, violates the terms and conditions of approval given by the competent Authority, engages in unfair practices or irregularities, or indulges in fraudulent practices.

Obligation to complete project u/s 8

In case of lapse or revocation of registration under section 7 of RERA, the Real Estate Regulatory Authority becomes obligated to complete the project.

Chapter 3

Rights of Allottees

1. Rights of the Allottees to obtain information

[SECTION 19(1)]

The allottee is entitled to obtain the information relating to sanctioned plans, layout plans, specifications approved by the Authority, and other information as provided in this Act, and the agreement for sale.

Corresponding Obligations on promoter

These rights of the allottees correspond to the promoter's obligations under 11(3)(a), under which the promoter is responsible for making the above information available to the allottee at the time the flat is booked and the allotment letter is issued.

Under section 11(1), the promoter must upload all the information about the project to the Authority at the time of registration and then regularly update the information, including the additional approvals received.

2. To know the stage-wise schedule of completion

[SECTION 19(2)]

The allottee shall be entitled to know the stage-wise project completion schedule, including the provisions for water, electricity, sanitation, other services as agreed between the promoter and the buyer per the terms and conditions of the agreement for sale.

Corresponding Obligations on the promoter

This right corresponds to the promoter's obligations under 11(3)(b), under which the promoter is responsible for making the above information available to the allottees at the time of booking and issue of the allotment letter.

3. To claim possession

[SECTION 19(3)]

The allottee is entitled to claim possession of the apartment, plot, or building. The association of allottees is entitled to claim the possession of the common areas, as a declaration is given by the promoter under section 4 of the Act.

Corresponding Obligations on the promoter

The affidavit and declaration in form B by the promoter when applying for registration of a real estate project are made binding, culminating in the rights of allottees u/s 19(3).

Section 17 of RERA requires the promoter to hand over possession and execute a conveyance deed of the common area in favour of the Association of Allottees.

4.To claim a refund in the event of non-completion

[SECTION 19(4)]

Section 19(4) of the Act states that the allottee is entitled to claim the refund of the amount with interest at a prescribed rate, If the promoter fails to comply or is unable to provide possession of the building, flat or apartment as per the terms of the sale agreement, or due to discontinuation of their business as a developer because of the suspension or revocation of their registration under this Act or the related rules and regulations, they shall be liable to pay compensation at the prescribed rate as provided under this Act.

Maha RERA Rule 19: Refund timelines

Promoters must make refunds, including any applicable interest and compensation under the Act or the Rules and Regulations, to allottees within thirty days from the date when such refund, interest, and compensation become due and payable to the allottee.

The concerned promoters are also required to report each instance within thirty days to the Authority.

Allottee has a right to claim compensation for the following reasons

Upon default by the promoter in handing over of possession:

- within the date specified in terms of the agreement of sale of the apartment
- or as per the specifications mentioned in the agreement for sale
- or the promoter discontinues his business as a developer.

5. To obtain documents and plans post-possession

[SECTION 19(5)]

The allottee shall be entitled to the necessary documents and plans, including those of common areas, after the promoter hands over physical possession of the building, plot or apartment.

Corresponding Obligations on the promoter

This right corresponds to section 11(1) of RERA, where the promoter has to upload all the project documents to the RERA website for the allottee's information.

Under section 17(2) of RERA, the promoter must hand over the documents of the apartment to the allottees and the common area to the association of allottees after handing over physical possession of the Apartment and the common area.

6. Right to get interest reduced when mutually agreed

[SECTION 19(8)]

Under sub-section (6), the obligations of the allottee and interest under sub-section (7) may be decreased through mutual agreement between the promoter and the allottee. Both parties have mutual rights and obligations. The allottee's responsibility to pay interest for delayed payment may be reduced through an agreement between the promoter and the allottee.

The Obligations of Promoters towards Allottees which translates into additional rights to Allottees:

Section 11 – transparency for allottees

Promoters have obligations towards allottees, which result in additional rights for allottees in the real estate regulatory framework. They are accountable for ensuring transparency and protecting allottees' interests. Project details will be created and regularly updated on the Authority's website as per Section 11(1). The Authority's website address must be included in all advertisements or prospectuses under Section 11(2). Allottees have the right to access specified documents and information under Section 11(3). Promoters are responsible for fulfilling all statutory obligations and functions until the conveyance of the project as per Section 11(4)(a), including addressing any structural or other defects.

Section 12 – liability on the Promoter

Promoters are held liable for false statements or misleading representations in advertisements or prospectuses. Allottees can claim compensation if they suffer a loss due to such misrepresentations according to Section 12.

Section 13 and 14

Promoters are prohibited from accepting more than 10% of the property's cost as an advance or application fee without a written agreement for sale with the allottee under Section 13.

Promoters must adhere to the approved plans and project specifications and can make changes only with the consent of the allottees. Additionally, the promoter is responsible for any structural defects within five years of possession as per Section 14.

Section 15 – Transfer to a third party

If the promoter transfers the project to a third party, the new promoter must adhere to all obligations and liabilities. The transfer requires written consent from two-thirds of the allottees and prior approval from the Regulatory Authority as stated in Section 15.

Section 16 - Insurance of Real Estate Project

Promoters must obtain insurance for the real estate project, including title insurance and construction insurance, to cover the project's land and buildings.

Section 17 - Transfer of Title

1. In the absence of local laws regarding the time limit for executing the conveyance deed, section 17 states that the Promoter shall transfer the title to the project within 3 months from the date

of issue of the oc. The promoter shall also be responsible for handing over the necessary documents and plans, including common areas, to the association of allottees or the competent Authority, as the case may be, within thirty days after obtaining the occupancy certificate.

2. The promoter shall ensure that a society is formed by the allottees within three months from the date of issue of the OC or after 51% of the allottees have paid full consideration to the promoter.
3. The association of the allottee or the allottee can approach RERA authorities to enforcement of the same.
4. In case of a violation of any of the provisions by the promoter, the allottee can file a complaint for compensation and/or enforcement of the same before the Authority. If the allottees' duties are not fulfilled, the promoter can approach the Authority to enforce the same.

Section 18 – Return of amount and compensation

This is the most important section for the claim of Interest and compensation under the RERA.

It deals with the promoter's obligations regarding compensation to the allottees (buyers) in case of delay or other issues. The key aspects of Section 18 are:

1. In the event of the project not being completed or possession of the property not being provided by the specified date, the buyer has the right to withdraw from the project. In such instances, the seller must refund the received amount with interest at a prescribed rate, along with compensation for any other incurred loss.
2. If the buyer chooses not to withdraw from the project, the seller is obligated to pay interest for each month of delay until possession is granted.
3. Should the seller fail to transfer the property title within the agreed time or if the title is flawed, the seller is accountable for compensating the buyer. There is no limit to the compensation amount in this scenario.

4. If the agreed-upon services are not provided as per the sale agreement, the seller must address the issue within 30 days of being notified. Failure to rectify the issue entitles the buyer to claim suitable compensation.

Chapter 4

Duties/Responsibilities of an Allottee

Responsibilities of Allottees to make payment

[SECTION 19(6)]

Each buyer who has consented to purchase an apartment, plot, or building, as applicable under section 13, is responsible for making the requisite payments as specified in the sale agreement. Additionally, the buyer must timely pay their share of registration charges, municipal taxes, water and electricity charges, maintenance charges, ground rent, and any other applicable charges as outlined in the agreement for sale. The payments must be made in the specified manner and timeframe as per the agreement for sale. E.g.

- Sale consideration as per stage-wise schedule of completion.
- Share of society formation and other charges at the time of possession.
- Water, electricity, and maintenance charges upon possession.

The promoter has the right u/s 11(5) of RERA to cancel the allotment in terms of the agreement for sale if the allottees do not make regular payments to the promoter as per the agreement. The obligation to make payment within the specified time and the associated liability may be reduced with mutual agreement between the promoter and allottee u/s 19(8).

To pay interest at a prescribed rate

[SECTION 19(7), MAHARERA RULE 18]

The allottee must pay interest, at the prescribed rate, for any delay in payment of any amount or charges under sub-section (6).

In accordance with Maha RERA, Rule 18, the rate of interest that is payable by the promoters to the allottees or vice versa shall be the State Bank of India's highest lending Rate plus two percent. If it is not in use, then it will be substituted by benchmark lending rates set by the State Bank of India from time to time for lending to the general public.

To contribute to the formation of a society/association

In accordance with SECTION 19(9), every homebuyer shall participate in the formation of an association, society, or cooperative society of the allottees or a federation of the same. The promoter has the right to compel the allottees to join the association to fulfill obligations under 11(4(e) of RERA to register the association of allottees upon booking the majority of the apartments.

To take timely physical possession

Every allottee is required to take physical possession of the flat, plot, or building within two months of the OC being issued for the said building, plot or apartment as per SECTION 19(10). The promoter has the right to compel the allottees to take possession of the apartment, plot, or building to comply with the obligation cast on him u/s 18 of RERA to complete the project and hand over the possession before the date agreed for possession as per the agreement for sale.

To participate in registering the conveyance deed

In adherence to SECTION 19(11), every allottee must participate in registering the conveyance deed of the apartment, plot, or building as per sub-section (1) of section 17 of the Act. The allottee is duty-bound to participate in the registration process and extend all cooperation. The promoter has the right to compel the allottee to participate in the conveyance process cast on him under section 17 to execute a registered conveyance deed of the building, apartment, or plot in favor of the allottee and of the undivided proportionate title in the common areas in favor of their association of allottees.

Penalty against allottee:

Penalty for failing to comply with orders of Authority by an allottee - Sections 67 and 68.

If the allottee fails to comply with or contravenes any order, decision, or direction of the RERA. In that case, they are liable to pay a penalty computed per day for the period during which the default goes on. The total penalty may extend up to 5% cumulatively of the cost of the building, apartment, or plot allotted to the allottee, as determined by the Authority. Furthermore, suppose the allottee fails to comply with or contravenes any order or direction of the Real Estate Appellate Tribunal. In that case, they can be imprisoned for up to one year or with a fine for each day during which the default continues, which may extend up to 10% of the cost of the building, apartment, or plot. In appropriate cases, the allottee may also be punished with imprisonment and a fine under Section 68 of the Real Estate (Regulation and Development) Act, 2016.

Chapter 5

Association of Allottees

RERA outlines the formation and functions of the association of allottees, which plays a crucial role in representing the interests of the property buyers in a real estate project.

Definition:

An association of allottees is a collective body formed by the buyers (allottees) of a real estate project. This association is intended to ensure that the buyer's rights and interests are protected and that the project's common areas and facilities are appropriately maintained.

Functions and Objectives:

1. Representation (Section 11(4)(e)):
   - Act as a representative body for all allottees to communicate and negotiate with the promoter or developer.
   - Address and resolve issues related to the project, including construction quality, possession delays, and legal matters.
2. Maintenance and Management (Section 11(4)(e)):
   - Oversee the maintenance and management of common areas, facilities, and amenities within the project.
   - Ensure the upkeep of roads, lighting, security, and landscaping.
3. Compliance and Legal Matters (Sections 17(1) and 17(2)):
   - Ensure compliance with the sale agreement terms, building norms, and other statutory requirements.
   - If necessary, take legal action to protect allottees' interests.
4. Financial Management (Sections 11(4)(e) and 19(6)):
   - Manage the collection and utilization of allottees' maintenance charges and other dues.
   - Maintain transparent financial records and ensure proper auditing.

5. Communication and Community Building (Section 11(4)(e)):
    - Facilitate communication among allottees through meetings, notices, and digital platforms.
    - Promote community building and organize social, cultural, or recreational activities for the residents.

Work to be Carried Out:

1. Formation and Registration (Section 11(4)(e)):
    - Legally form and register the association per local laws and regulations.
    - Draft and adopt a constitution or bylaws that govern the functioning of the association.
2. Regular Meetings (Section 11(4)(e)):
    - Conduct regular meetings to discuss and address various issues related to the project.
    - Ensure participation and consensus-building among all allottees.
3. Liaison with Promoter (Sections 11(4)(d) and 17(1) and 17(2)):
    - Coordinate with the promoter to ensure timely project completion and compliance with agreed terms.
    - Monitor the handover process of common areas and ensure all necessary documents and plans are received.
4. Dispute Resolution (Section 19(6)):
    - Address and resolve disputes among allottees or between allottees and the promoter.
    - Mediate conflicts and ensure harmonious living conditions within the community.

Importance for an Allottee:

1. Protection of Rights (Section 11(4)(e)):
    - The association ensures that the rights of allottees are protected and that they have a collective voice when dealing with the promoter.

2. Accountability (Sections 11(4)(d) and 17(1)):
   - Promoters are accountable for their commitments, ensuring that construction standards, deadlines, and legal requirements are met.
3. Maintenance and Upkeep (Section 17(2)):
   - Ensures proper common areas and facilities maintenance, enhancing living conditions and property value.
4. Transparency (Sections 11(4)(e) and 19(6)):
   - Promotes financial transparency and accountability in collecting and utilizing maintenance charges and other funds.
5. Community Living (Section 11(4)(e)):
   - Facilitates better community living by organizing social events, resolving disputes, and fostering a sense of belonging among residents.

As outlined in RERA, the association of allottees is a fundamental entity that empowers property buyers. It ensures that their investment is secure and that their living environment is well-maintained and managed.

Project Completion by Association of Allottees under Maha RERA

The Maharashtra Real Estate Regulatory Authority (Maha RERA) provides a framework that empowers the association of allottees to complete stalled projects in case the promoter fails to do so. This mechanism ensures that the rights and investments of allottees are protected and that the project reaches completion. Below is a detailed explanation of how this process works:

1. Legal Framework and Triggering Conditions

Section 8 of RERA:

The Regulatory Authority can intervene if a promoter fails to complete a project. Maha RERA may pass an order allowing the association of allottees to take over and complete the project.

Conditions for Triggering Section 8:

- Significant delays in project completion beyond the agreed timeline.
- Insolvency or bankruptcy of the promoter.
- Revocation or lapse of the promoter's registration due to non-compliance with statutory obligations.

2. Empowerment of the Association of Allottees

Once Maha RERA identifies that the promoter cannot complete the project, it can empower the association of allottees to step in. This includes providing legal Authority and administrative support necessary for project completion.

3. Steps for Project Completion by the Association of Allottees

Assessment and Planning:

The association first comprehensively assesses the project's status, including construction progress, financial health, and compliance with regulatory requirements. Then, a detailed project completion plan is developed, outlining timelines, budgets, and responsibilities.

Appointment of Professionals:

The association may appoint professionals such as project managers, engineers, architects, and legal advisors to ensure efficient project completion. These professionals help manage construction activities, obtain necessary approvals, and ensure compliance with legal and safety standards.

Financial Management:

The association takes over the financial management of the project, which includes:

- Collecting pending dues from allottees.
- Manage existing funds and arrange additional financing if required.

- Ensuring transparent and accountable use of funds for project-related expenses.

Engagement with Contractors and Vendors:

To resume construction work, the association may need to renegotiate or enter into new contracts with contractors and vendors. It ensures that all agreements are fair, transparent, and in the best interest of the allottees.

Compliance and Approvals:

Throughout the completion process, the association ensures compliance with all regulatory requirements, including obtaining approvals and local authorities' clearances.

4. Role of Maha RERA

Monitoring and Support:

Maha RERA continuously monitors the project's progress under the association's management. It provides necessary support and guidance to resolve any issues arising during the completion process.

Dispute Resolution:

In any disputes between the association and allottees or with external parties, Maha RERA acts as an adjudicating authority to resolve conflicts and ensure smooth project execution.

5. Benefits to Allottees

Project Completion:

The primary benefit is the completion of the stalled project, which will ensure that allottees finally receive their apartments or plots.

Protection of Investments:

By taking over the project, the association safeguards the financial investments of allottees and prevents further economic loss.

Transparency and Accountability:

The association's management ensures high transparency and accountability in project execution, fostering trust among allottees.

Community Building:

As the association represents the interests of all allottees, it promotes a sense of community and collective responsibility, leading to better cooperation and harmony among residents.

In case the Association of Allottees is not willing to take over and complete the project, the Maha RERA can enforce the implementation of the stalled projects through a new developer or a State Government Development Authority like MHADA, MMRDA, CICDO, etc.

Chapter 6

Revocation of Registration

Revocation, in the context of the Real Estate (Regulation and Development) Act, 2016 (RERA), refers to the cancellation of a real estate project's registration by the Real Estate Regulatory Authority. This action is taken when the promoter fails to comply with the registration terms and conditions or violates the provisions of the Act.

What is Revocation?

Revocation is the formal withdrawal of the approval and registration granted to a real estate project by the regulatory Authority. It is a legal remedy available under RERA to protect the homebuyers interests and ensure that the real estate market operates transparently and fairly.

When can a registration be revoked?

Under the Act, the registration of a real estate project can be revoked by the Real Estate Regulatory Authority on several grounds as mentioned in Section 7:

1. Default by Promoter (Section 7(1)(a)):

If the promoter violates the terms and conditions of the approvals given by any competent Authority or the terms or conditions of the project registration.

2. Misrepresentation or Fraud (Section 7(1)(b)):

If the promoter indulges in any kind of unfair practice or irregularities, including misleading advertisements, false statements about the project, and fraud.

3. Delay in Project (Section 7(1)(c)):

If the promoter is unable to give possession, or is unable to complete the project as per the terms of the sale agreement or the approved plans.

4. Violation of Laws (Section 7(1)(d)):

The promoter violates any other obligations under the Act or the rules and regulations made thereunder.

Consequences of Revocation

When a registration is revoked, it leads to several significant consequences as outlined in Section 8 and related provisions of RERA:

1. Public Notice (Section 7(3)):

The Authority must issue a public notice about the revocation.

2. Freezing of Bank Accounts (Section 7(4)(a)):

The Authority has the power to direct that the project's bank accounts be frozen.

3. Transfer of Project (Section 8):

The Authority can consult with the appropriate government to take necessary action, which may include a competent authority or any association of allottees carrying out the remaining development work or designating another developer to complete the project.

After Revocation: Promoter's Point of View

1. Loss of Control:

The promoter loses control over the project, and the development rights are handed over to the Authority or another designated entity.

2. Financial Implications:

The promoter may face significant financial losses. Their bank accounts related to the project can be frozen, and they may be required to compensate for delays and defects.

3. Reputation Damage:

The revocation severely damages the promoter's reputation, impacting future projects and credibility in the real estate market.

4. Legal Consequences:

The promoter may face further legal action for breaches of the Act, including penalties and potential imprisonment under Sections 59 and 60 of RERA.

After Revocation: Allottees and Association of Allottees' Point of View

1. Protection of Interests:

The allottees' interests are prioritized. The Authority ensures the project is completed as per the original terms or in a revised manner that meets statutory and contractual obligations.

2. Financial Security:

The funds from the frozen accounts are safeguarded and used to complete the project. The association of allottees may be involved in managing these funds under the supervision of the Authority (Section 8).

3. Completion of Project:

A competent authority or another developer takes over the project to ensure its completion. This might lead to some delays, but the objective is to protect the allottees' investments (Section 8).

4. Involvement in Decision Making:

The association of allottees may play an active role in decision-making and liaising with the new developer or competent Authority to ensure the project meets the required standards (Section 8).

5. Recourse and Redressal:

Allottees have a clear path to seek compensation from the promoter for delays, defects, and other grievances through the Authority (Sections 12, 18, and 19).

Chapter 7

Stalled Projects and their Revival

A stalled project is a real estate project that is not functional or active and is not in a position to meet the commitments given to the Allottees.

The RERA Act has addressed the subject of "Stalled Projects" by making multiple provisions in the interest of the Allottees.

Various reasons have been identified that result in a real estate project becoming a stalled project:

(i) Mala fide intent of Promoters

(ii) Diversion of Funds by the promoters

(iii) Siphoning of Funds by the Promoters

(iv) Lack of response from the market

(v) Internal disputes between the Promoters

(vi) Litigations in land acquisition

(vii) Dispute with landowners

(viii) Delay in obtaining approvals, sanctions, and permission from concerned authorities

(ix) Lack of or delay in obtaining project finance

(x) Improper Financial closure of the project resulting in inadequate funding

The Maharashtra Real Estate Regulatory Authority has taken several proactive measures to address and resolve stalled real estate projects effectively.

Below is a detailed explanation of Maha RERA's approach:

1. Project Management System (Section 34(f))

Implementation of a Robust Tracking System:

Maha RERA has developed a comprehensive project management system that tracks the progress of all registered real estate projects. This system includes detailed timelines, milestones, and financial aspects of each project. Promoters must submit regular updates and submissions to keep the system current, allowing the Authority to monitor progress and identify potential delays early.

2. Resolution Panels (Section 32(g))

Establishment of Dedicated Panels:

Maha RERA has set up specialized resolution panels comprising real estate, legal, and financial experts. These panels promptly address disputes and issues related to stalled projects, providing a structured mechanism for conflict resolution.

3. Interim Relief Measures (Section 37)

Providing Immediate Support to Allottees:

Maha RERA offers interim relief to affected allottees, such as compensation for delays or temporary housing arrangements, to mitigate the impact of project stalling. These measures are designed to provide immediate support while long-term solutions are being worked out.

4. Stakeholder Meetings (Section 34(e))

Facilitating Collaborative Solutions:

Regular meetings are conducted with all stakeholders, including promoters, allottees, financial institutions, and government bodies. These meetings aim to facilitate open communication, identify bottlenecks, and collaboratively develop solutions to expedite project completion.

5. Enforcement of Penalties and Sanctions (Section 7(3))

Ensuring Accountability and Compliance:

Maha RERA enforces strict penalties and sanctions on promoters who fail to comply with project timelines and other statutory obligations.

These penalties include monetary fines, freezing of bank accounts, and even revocation of project registration in severe cases.

6. Appointment of Administrator or Co-promoter (Section 8)

Involving Competent Entities to Complete Projects:

When a promoter cannot complete the project, Maha RERA may appoint an administrator or a co-promoter to take over and complete the project. This ensures that the project progresses under competent management and aligns with regulatory requirements.

7. Financial Audits and Transparency (Section 11(4)(g))

Ensuring Proper Utilization of Funds:

Maha RERA conducts thorough financial audits of stalled projects to ensure that the funds collected from homebuyers are utilized appropriately. Promoters must maintain transparent financial records and provide regular updates to the Authority and allottees.

8. Public Disclosure and Communication (Section 34(b))

Maintaining Transparency and Keeping Allottees Informed:

Maha RERA maintains a public portal where the status of all registered projects is disclosed. This portal includes details on project progress, financial status, and any issues faced. Regular communication is ensured with allottees to keep them informed about the steps to resolve the stalling issues and the expected timelines for project completion.

9. Legal Recourse and Support (Section 31)

Providing Legal Support to Allottees:

Maha RERA offers legal support and guidance to allottees to help them understand their rights and the legal remedies available. This includes assistance in filing complaints and seeking compensation or refunds where applicable.

10. Hearings by the Authority (Section 35)

Conducting Formal Hearings:

MahaRERA conducts formal hearings to address complaints and disputes related to stalled projects. During these hearings, all parties involved, including the promoter and allottees, present their case. Based on the findings, the authority issues orders and directions to ensure that the project progresses and that all stakeholder interests are safeguarded. These hearings ensure due process and fair resolution of issues.

Chapter 8

Unfair Practices by Promoters

1. Issue of unsigned booking forms and incomplete allotment letters.
2. Not sharing the draft of the agreement for sale before booking.
3. Sharing the draft agreement of sale only after booking.
4. Collecting non-refundable and forfeitable money as a booking amount from prospective buyers, even before entering into an agreement for sale.
5. Collection of booking amount without full disclosure of the date of possession and proper approvals, such as a commencement certificate.
6. In Phases 1 and 2, allottees were promised amenities like a clubhouse, which will most likely be completed after Phase 3.
7. The promoter does not accept any suggestions/recommendations requested by the allottees in the agreement for sale, forcing the allottees to sign on the dotted lines.
8. Bringing final printed papers of the agreement for sale directly to the registration office for signing and registration without sharing the draft.
9. Collecting high legal expenses for entering basic, stereotype, and cyclostyled agreements for sale between the Promoter and allottee.
10. Collecting more than 10% of money without registration of agreement of sale.
11. Collecting money more than 10% entering into a Memorandum of Understanding.
12. Collecting 90-100% of the money initially under the garb of offering steep discounts.

And many more.

Chapter 9

AIF and SWAMIH Funds

An Alternative Investment Fund (AIF) in India refers to any fund established in India that is a privately pooled investment vehicle that takes funds from sophisticated investors, whether Indian or foreign and invests them following a defined investment policy for the benefit of its investors. AIFs are presided over by SEBI, under the SEBI (AIF) Regulations, 2012.

Alternative Investment Funds (AIFs) can significantly assist homebuyers, especially in the context of the Real Estate (Regulation and Development) Act, 2016 (RERA).

1. Funding Stalled Projects

Problem: Post-RERA, many real estate projects have been stalled due to developers' financial difficulties, leaving homebuyers in a lurch.

Solution: AIFs, especially Category II funds (like real estate funds), can provide the necessary funding to revive and complete these stalled projects. This ensures that homebuyers receive their homes without further delays. These funds often provide last-mile financing, which is crucial for project completion.

2. Ensuring Compliance and Transparency

Problem: Homebuyers often face issues related to the lack of transparency and delayed delivery from developers.

Solution: AIFs bring professionalism and stringent compliance to their investment projects. They ensure that developers adhere to RERA regulations, including project registration, timely updates, and transparency in using funds. This increases homebuyer confidence and trust in the projects financed by AIFs.

3. Providing Financial Stability to Developers

Problem: The financial instability of developers can lead to project delays and failure to meet RERA obligations.

Solution: By providing equity or debt financing, AIFs can stabilize developers' financial positions, ensuring that projects have the necessary funds to proceed as planned. This financial backing helps developers meet RERA-mandated deadlines and maintain project quality, ultimately benefiting homebuyers.

4. Supporting Affordable Housing Projects

Problem: There is a high demand for affordable housing, but developers often lack the financial resources to undertake such projects.

Solution: Category I AIFs, such as social venture funds, can focus on affordable housing projects and ensure that they receive the required capital. These funds can help developers launch and complete projects to provide affordable housing, aligning with RERA's objective of increasing housing availability and affordability.

5. Facilitating Secondary Market Transactions

Problem: Homebuyers sometimes need to exit their investments for personal financial reasons, but the secondary market for under-construction properties is underdeveloped.

Solution: AIFs can facilitate secondary market transactions by buying out existing homebuyers who need liquidity. This provides an exit option for homebuyers and maintains the liquidity of the real estate market. Such actions by AIFs also help maintain project momentum by ensuring that financial resources remain available.

6. Expertise and Due Diligence

Problem: Homebuyers may not have the expertise to evaluate real estate projects' financial health and reliability.

Solution: AIFs conduct thorough due diligence before investing in real estate projects. Their expertise in assessing the viability and risk of projects ensures that only those with strong potential for completion and compliance with RERA are funded. This indirectly benefits homebuyers by increasing the likelihood of successful project completion.

7. Post-Completion Support

Problem: Post-completion, developers might fail to manage the property efficiently, affecting homebuyers' living experience.

Solution: Some AIFs invest in the construction phase and support post-completion management. They ensure that projects are well-maintained and managed according to best practices, enhancing the living conditions for homebuyers.

SWAMIH Funds

The SWAMIH (Special Window for Affordable and Mid-Income Housing) Fund was established by the Indian government to address the problem of stalled housing projects and to provide relief to homebuyers.

What is the SWAMIH Fund?

Objective: The primary goal of the SWAMIH Fund is to provide last-mile funding to stalled residential projects, particularly those in the affordable and mid-income housing segments. These projects are often delayed due to financial constraints, leaving homebuyers in a lurch.

Category: It is a Category II Alternative Investment Fund (AIF) as per SEBI regulations.

Manager: SBICAP Ventures Ltd, a wholly-owned subsidiary of the State Bank of India, manages the fund.

Capital: The fund was initially launched with a corpus of INR 25,000 crores, with contributions from both the government and various financial institutions.

How Does the SWAMIH Fund Work?

1. Funding Stalled Projects:

The fund provides financial support to real estate projects that are stuck due to last-mile funding issues. These are projects that are in advanced stages of construction but cannot progress due to a lack of funds.

2. Project Eligibility:

- Projects must be registered under RERA.
- They should be affordable and mid-income housing projects.
- The project should be net worth positive.
- The construction should be completed significantly, usually at least 30%.

3. Application Process:

Developers can apply for funding through SBICAP Ventures Ltd. The applications are scrutinized based on project viability, completion stage, sales track record, and more.

How SWAMIH Fund Assists Homebuyers under RERA

1. Ensuring Timely Completion: By providing the necessary funds to complete stalled projects, the SWAMIH Fund helps ensure homebuyers promptly receive possession of their homes. This mitigates the risk of indefinite delays.
2. RERA Compliance: Since only RERA-registered projects are eligible for funding, homebuyers are protected under the RERA framework, which mandates timely delivery, transparency, and accountability from developers.
3. Protection Against Financial Stress: Homebuyers who have invested in delayed projects face significant financial and emotional stress. The SWAMIH Fund's intervention helps alleviate this by resuming and completing the construction.
4. Legal Recourse: If the SWAMIH Fund funds a project and still faces issues, homebuyers have a structured legal recourse under RERA to address grievances, ensuring better protection of their rights.
5. Market Stability: By reviving stalled projects, the SWAMIH Fund also helps stabilize the real estate market, ensuring that

housing investments remain safe and that trust in the sector is maintained.

For more information about SWAMIH funds, refer to 'The SWAMIH Story' by Irfan A. Kazi.

Part 3
Promoters Corner

Chapter 1

Promoter under RERA

Section 2(zk) of the Act states that

A promoter in real estate encompasses a variety of roles and responsibilities. This includes individuals or entities who construct or cause the construction of independent buildings or apartments intending to sell them to others and those who develop the land into projects for the same purpose, regardless of whether they also build structures on the plots. Additionally, development authorities or public bodies are considered promoters when they construct buildings or sell plots on land owned by them or provided by the Government. Apex State-level cooperative housing finance societies and primary cooperative housing societies that construct apartments for their members also fall under this definition. Furthermore, any individual acting as a builder, colonizer, contractor, developer, or estate developer, or those claiming to hold a power of attorney from the landowner, are considered promoters. Lastly, anyone constructing buildings or apartments for sale to the public is also categorized as a promoter, highlighting the broad spectrum of parties involved in real estate development and sales.

Explanation

A promoter in the context of real estate projects is defined as any individual or entity involved in the development and sale of properties. Specifically, when one party is responsible for constructing or converting a building into apartments or developing a plot for sale, while another party is responsible for selling those apartments or plots, both parties are deemed promoters. They share joint liability for fulfilling the functions and responsibilities outlined under the Act and its associated rules and regulations. Additionally, Maha RERA Circular Nos. 12 and 13, dated 4th December 2017, extend the definition of a promoter to include landowners or investors who possess a share of the project area or revenue. This means that all stakeholders in a real estate project, including landowners and investors, are subject to the same obligations and accountability, ensuring comprehensive compliance and responsibility throughout the development process.

The Bombay High Court's ruling in Nayan Shah and Others vs. Apex Buildwell Pvt. Ltd. and Others highlights this.

In this case, the court examined the relationship between the landowner and the developer. It concluded that landowners who enter into development agreements with builders or developers will be treated as promoters under RERA. The court reasoned that since the landowners are part of the project and benefit from the sale of the property, they share the responsibilities and liabilities towards the allottees and the developer.

A judicial ruling where an Assignee is considered a promoter is the case of M/s. Paradise Builders Pvt. Ltd. vs. The State of Maharashtra & Ors., heard by the Bombay High Court.

A very famous case concerns Lavasa Corporation Limited. It involved a case in which the person who provides the apartments on a long lease is also a promoter.

Functions and duties of the Promoter

The duties of the Promoter are

1. To get the real estate project registered under RERA
2. To observe only the concept of 'carpet area' in all transactions
3. To submit all relevant information about the project in the form of an affidavit
4. To deposit 70% of the amount received by the Allottees to the RERA-designated bank account
5. To declare the time of completion of the project at the time of registration
6. To disclose correct and factual information on the Maha RERA website
7. To make available to the Allottee all vital information and an issue of the Allotment letter

8. To be responsible for all obligations and responsibilities as per the agreement of sale
9. To obtain the completion/occupancy certificate
10. To obtain the lease certificate
11. To provide essential maintenance services
12. To form an Association of Allottees
13. To execute conveyance in favour of the association of allottees
14. To pay all the outgoings of the project
15. To abstain from creating any lien or mortgage on property sold to an allottee and to protect the rights of the allottee
16. To prepare and maintain all project details
17. To remain committed to the veracity of the advertisement
18. To not take any deposit or advance from the Allottee before entering into an agreement of sale
19. To adhere to sanctioned plans and project specifications
20. To fulfil obligations in case of a transfer of the project to a third party
21. To get the real estate project insured
22. To execute conveyance
23. To refund the amount paid by the allottee in case of any default

Usage of only Carpet area by the Promoter

Section 2(k) of the act states

"Carpet area means the net usable floor area of an apartment, excluding the area covered by the external walls, areas under services shafts, exclusive balcony or veranda areas and exclusive open terrace areas, but includes the area covered by the internal partition walls of the apartment."

Explanation

In this clause, the term "exclusive balcony or veranda area" refers to the specific area of a balcony or veranda attached to the net usable area of a flat and designated for the exclusive use of the allottee. Similarly, "exclusive open terrace area" denotes the area of an open terrace associated with an apartment's net usable floor area, intended solely for the allottee's use. The primary rationale behind RERA's emphasis on using only the carpet area is to standardize and regulate the real estate sector. This approach prevents promoters from utilizing terms such as built-up area, usable area, super built-up area, and saleable area in their documentation. By focusing on the carpet area, RERA aims to enhance buyer trust in promoters and achieve its core objective of promoting transparency within the real estate sector.

Chapter 2

Registering the Project with RERA

Section 3(1) of RERA states that –

A promoter must register a project that is greater than 500 sq. m. in size and has more than eight apartments. The Promoter is prohibited from marketing and advertising the project before completing all the required due diligence.

If the Promoter commits any violations during the registration process, he may be charged with either a penalty, which may amount to 10% of the total cost of the project, or he may be imprisoned for up to 3 years. He may also be charged with both. The Authority can also revoke the registration of the project if he commits any fraudulent activities or violates any terms given by the Authority.

Suppose any complaint is filed against the Promoter by any aggrieved party. In that case, he is liable to refund the amount the party paid or compensate them with compensation, as decided by the Authority.

The text also mentions that promoters are prohibited from promoting, advertising, booking, selling, or inviting individuals to purchase any property in a real estate project without first registering the real estate project with RERA.

Provided that projects that are ongoing on the date of commencement of this Act and for which the completion certificate has not been issued, the Promoter shall make an application to the Authority for registration of the said project within a period of three months from the date of commencement of this Act:

Provided further that if the Authority thinks necessary, in the interest of allottees, for projects which are developed beyond the planning area but with the requisite permission of the Local Authority, it may, by order, direct the Promoter of such project to register with the Authority. The provisions of this Act, or the rules and regulations made thereunder, shall apply to such projects from that registration stage.

For matters when registration is not required, RERA in section (2) of the Act states that, no registration of a real estate project is required under the following conditions:

(a) When the land area intended for development does not exceed five hundred square meters.

(b) When the total number of apartments proposed for development does not exceed eight, including all phases.

Provided that the appropriate Government may choose to lower these thresholds below five hundred square meters or eight apartments for exemption from registration under this Act.

(c) When the promoter has already received a cc for a real estate project before the commencement of this Act.

(d) For projects involving renovation, repair, or redevelopment that do not include marketing, advertising, or a new sale/allotment of an apartment.

Section 2(zn) of the Act defines a real estate project in the following manner

Real Estate Project: A 'Real Estate Project' refers to the development of a structure consisting of apartments, the conversion of an existing building or a part of it into apartments, or the development of land into plots or apartments, with the intent to sell all or some of the said apartments, plots, or buildings. This definition encompasses common areas, development works, all improvements and structures on the site, and all associated easements, rights, and appurtenances.

Planning Area: A 'Planning Area' denotes any area designated as a planning area, development area, local planning area, or regional development plan area, regardless of its name, as specified by the appropriate Government or any competent authority. This includes any area identified by the relevant Government or competent Authority for future planned development under the prevailing law related to town and country planning, including any revisions made to such designations over time.

Section 4 of RERA states that

The registration of the project should be carried out by professionals. If this is not done, there is a high chance that discrepancies could exist in the registration, which would result in the Promoter being charged fines or penalties. The Promoter must hire well-trained CAs, Advocates, Engineers, and Architects who are experienced in the field of Real Estate.

Registration under RERA requires a promoter to register every one of their projects. They can also register a single project in phases with different completion dates. It could be carried out either tower-wise or wing-wise, as the Promoter chooses. The entire registration process occurs online on the Maha RERA website by filling out an application, where all the required documents must be uploaded.

Maha RERA allows phase-wise registration of projects. This form of registration has the advantages of reducing the penalty levied, securing the balance in the RERA-designated account early, and easing planning, execution, and completion. The different phases can also have different completion dates.

However, it would increase compliance, due diligence, designated accounts, GST registrations, etc.

They also allow wing-wise registration and floor-wise registration, both of which have advantages and disadvantages and specific circumstances in which they can be used.

For registrations of projects where some of the units have already been sold, the Promoter must disclose them in Form 3, which is to be filled out by the appointed Chartered Accountant.

Procedure to extend the period of registration

1. Application for Extension

According to Section 6 of the Act, RERA can extend the registration upon an application made by the Promoter due to force majeure. The application must be submitted in a specified form and accompanied by a fee as prescribed by the regulations established by the Authority.

2. Grounds for Extension

In reasonable circumstances and without any default on the part of the Promoter, the Authority may extend the registration granted for a period deemed necessary, not exceeding one year in total. It is important to note that no application for extension shall be rejected without allowing the applicant to be heard regarding the matter. Here, 'Force Majeure' is defined as any extraordinary event or circumstance that hinders the Promoter from fulfilling their contractual obligations. Examples of such events include natural disasters (e.g., floods, earthquakes), wars, riots, and extraordinary circumstances such as the Covid-19 pandemic.

3. Application Submission and Fee Structure

Per Section 7 of the Act, an application for extending the real estate project must be made to the Authority in Form "E". The application should include an explanatory note outlining the grounds and reasons for the delay in project completion, along with supporting documentation.

4. Granting or Rejecting the Application

The Authority will grant the extension of registration in Form "F" and provide a copy to the Promoter. If the application for extension is rejected, the Authority shall inform the Promoter in Form "D" after allowing the applicant to be heard, as stipulated in the second proviso of Section 6. The notification shall also be sent to the respective competent and statutory authorities.

5. Fee Calculation

The application for extension of the real estate project must include a fee based on the area of land intended for development, calculated at a rate of ⊡10 per square meter. The minimum payment is ten thousand rupees, and the maximum is ten lakh rupees. The fee shall be calculated at ⊡5 per square meter for plotted developments.

6. Consequences of Non-Application

Should the Promoter fail to submit an application for extension, the Authority may impose restrictions on the advertisement and marketing of the project. Consequently, the Promoter would be unable to sell any apartments, and all loans to the Promoter and allottees would be halted. This could lead to reputational damage for the Promoter, disassociation of professionals from the project, and classification of the project as 'lapsed.' Moreover, allottees may withdraw from the project, potentially leading to the association of allottees taking over the project.

Procedure for Registration of Real Estate Projects

1. Application for Registration

Section 4 of the Real Estate (Regulation and Development) Act (RERA) mandates that every Promoter submit an application to the Authority for the registration of a real estate project. This application must be completed in a prescribed form, manner, and timeframe and should be accompanied by the required fee as specified by the regulations set forth by the Authority.

2. Authority's Response

The Authority must respond within thirty days of receiving the application as per subsection (1). The possible actions include:

a. Grant of Registration: The Authority may grant registration in accordance with the provisions of the Act, rules, and regulations. The applicant will be issued a registration number, along with a Login ID and password, allowing access to the Authority's website to create a web page to input details of the proposed project.

b. Rejection of Application: Should the application not comply with the provisions of the Act or the accompanying regulations, it may be rejected. However, no application shall be denied without allowing the applicant to present their case.

3. Deemed Registration

The project will be registered automatically if the Authority does not grant or reject the application within thirty days. The Authority is then required to issue a registration number, Login ID, and password to the Promoter within seven days following the initial thirty-day expiration.

4. Validity of Registration

The registration granted under this section will remain valid for the duration declared by the Promoter concerning the completion of the project or any specific phase thereof.

5. Appeals Against Rejection

In the event that the Authority rejects a project's registration, the Promoter has the right to appeal before the Appellate Tribunal within sixty working days of receiving the rejection order.

Documentation Required with Application

Section 4 of the Act and Rule 3 of Maha RERA states that -

1. Information and Documentation Requirements

The Promoter must submit the following information and documents for the registration of the real estate project, as stipulated by the Act:

a. Enterprise Details:

- Name, registered address, and type of the enterprise (e.g., proprietorship, partnership, company).
- Registration particulars and the names and photographs of the Promoter or authorized representatives.

b. Personal Identification:

- Authenticated copy of the Promoter's Permanent Account Number (PAN) card.
- For individual Promoters, include their name, photograph, contact details, and address. For corporate entities, provide similar information for the chairman, partners, directors, and authorized representatives.

c. Previous Projects:

- Summary of projects launched in the past five years, detailing their current status, any delays, pending legal cases, and relevant land types and payment statuses.

d. Legal Title Documentation:

- A legal title report verifying ownership of the land proposed for development, authenticated by a practising advocate.
- If the Promoter is not the landowner, include copies of collaboration, development, or joint development agreements reflecting the owner's consent and authenticated legal title reports concerning any encumbrances on the land.

e. Pending Legal Proceedings:

- Details of any ongoing legal proceedings affecting the land intended for development.

f. Project Plans and Details:

- Sanctioned plans, layout plans, and specifications for the proposed project, including approved phases.
- Information on Floor Space Index (FSI), Transferable Development Rights (TDR), and amenities in accordance with applicable Development Control Regulations.
- Proposed number of buildings, floors, and changes during the project's progression, including aggregate areas for recreational open space and covered parking spaces.

g. Development Plan:

- A comprehensive plan for development works, including provisions for firefighting, drinking water, emergency evacuation, and renewable energy usage.

h. Allotment Documentation:

- Samples of the allotment letter, agreement for sale, and conveyance deed proposed for signing with allottees.

i. Project Specifications:

- Information regarding the number, type, and carpet area of apartments for sale, including areas of exclusive balconies, verandas, or open terraces.
- Details about the number and sizes of garages available for sale within the project.

j. Development Team:

- Names and addresses of contractors, architects, structural engineers, and other professionals associated with the project.

k. Legal Declaration:

- A signed affidavit by the Promoter or an authorized representative stating:
- Legal title to the land proposed for development, along with valid documentation.

- Assurance that the land is free from encumbrances or details of any existing encumbrances.
- Commitment regarding the timeline for project completion.
- Declaration that 70% of funds received from allottees will be deposited in a separate bank account for project costs, with withdrawals based on the project's percentage of completion, certified by qualified professionals.
- Confirmation that accounts will be audited annually by a chartered accountant to ensure proper utilization of funds.

2. Application Form

The application for registration must be made in **Form 'A'**, submitted in writing by the Promoter or an authorized representative, and must be submitted in triplicate.

3. Online Application Submission

Once the Authority establishes provisions for web-based applications, the requirement for triplicate submissions will be waived.

4. Registration Fee

At the time of application, the Promoter is required to pay a registration fee based on the area of land proposed for development:

- **₹10 per square meter**, with a minimum fee of **₹10,000** and a maximum fee of **₹10 lakhs.**
- For plotted developments, the fee is **₹5 per square meter.**
- Payment should be made through NEFT, RTGS, or other digital transaction modes.

5. Declaration Requirement

A declaration, as specified under sub-clause (1) of sub-section (2) of section 4, must be submitted in **Form "B"**.

6. Withdrawal of Application

The Promoter may withdraw their application for registration within **30 days** of submission. The registration fee will be retained as administrative charges, and the remaining balance will be refunded according to regulations set by the Authority.

7. Cost Disclosure

The Promoter must disclose the following:

- Land cost for the project.
- Construction cost for the project.
- Estimated total cost of the real estate project as defined in the Act.

Self-Regulatory Organisations –

As per Order no. 10 of Maha RERA, dated 11th October 2019, obtaining membership to any of the SROs has become compulsory before the application for registration for the Real Estate Project with Maha RERA. A promoter can join any SRO, such as CREDAI Maharashtra, NAREDCO, MBVA, BAI, BDA or CREDAI- MCHI.

RERA-designated bank account

1. Separate Bank Account Requirement

Under Section 4 of the Act, the Promoter must maintain a separate bank account exclusively for transactions related to a specific real estate project. This account must contain **70%** of the funds received from allottees for the project. The purpose of this requirement is to:

- Prevent the diversion of funds by the Promoter to other projects.
- Ensure transparency in working capital management.
- Avoid project delays resulting from mismanagement of funds.

2. Declaration and Affidavit

As per Section 4(2)(l)(D) of the Act, the Promoter or an authorized representative must provide a declaration, supported by an affidavit, stating that:

- **70%** of the amounts received from allottees will be deposited in a separate account maintained at a scheduled bank. This account will be used solely to cover construction and land costs.
- Withdrawals from this account must be proportional to the percentage of project completion, as certified by an engineer, architect, and chartered accountant.

3. Withdrawal Conditions

- The Promoter can withdraw funds from the separate account only to cover the project costs, which are aligned with the percentage of project completion.
- The calculation for the percentage of completion is defined as:
- Percentage of Completion=(Amount incurred on land cost and constructionEstimated project cost of land and construction)×100%\text{Percentage of Completion} = \left(\frac{\text{Amount incurred on land cost and construction}}{\text{Estimated project cost of land and construction}} \right) \times 100\%Percentage of Completion=(Estimated project cost of land and constructionAmount incurred on land cost and construction)×100%

4. Use of Remaining Funds

The remaining **30%** can be deposited in any bank account and withdrawn without restrictions. However, withdrawals from this account must still be used solely for project-related costs, adhering to the completion percentage.

5. Scheduled Bank Requirement

The separate account must be opened in a **scheduled bank**, which refers to banks in the 2nd schedule of the RBI Act, comprising both Commercial Banks and Scheduled Co-operative Banks.

6. Annual Audit and Reporting

To ensure oversight of the Promoter's financial activities:

- The Promoter must have their accounts audited by a chartered accountant within six months after the end of each financial year. The auditor must verify that the funds collected for the project have been utilized accordingly.
- An annual report on the statement of accounts must be uploaded to the **Maha RERA** website within the specified timeframe.

7. Penalties for Non-Compliance

In cases of non-compliance, the Promoter may face penalties under Section 60/63 of the Act, which could be up to **5%** of the project's cost. The Authority also has the power to periodically audit the bank accounts, with the Promoter bearing the audit costs.

8. Authority's Power to Freeze Accounts

In the event of project revocation, the Authority can freeze the separate bank account and take necessary actions. All transactions within this account must adhere to the norms established in the Act, and each withdrawal should be supported by a request letter from the Promoter, attested by an authorized signatory.

Quarterly progress reports

1. Webpage Creation and Updates

Under Section 11 of the Act, once the Promoter receives a Login ID and password, they must create a webpage on the Authority's website. This page must include all relevant details of the proposed project as specified under Section 4(2) and be updated quarterly to provide the public with transparent information. The required updates include:

- **Registration Details:** Information regarding the registration granted by the Authority.
- **Booking Updates:** A quarterly list of the number and types of apartments or plots booked.
- **Garage Booking Updates:** A quarterly list of garages booked.
- **Approvals:** A list of obtained and pending approvals is updated quarterly after the commencement certificate.
- **Project Status:** A quarterly update on the status of the project.
- **Additional Information:** Any other information and documents specified by the regulations made by the Authority.

2. Requirement for Timely Updates

The Promoter is responsible for updating various project details, including:

- New permissions received.
- Progress of construction.
- Changes in project details.

- Updates on project costs.
- Any other relevant information.

For significant changes in project information, the Promoter must seek prior approval from the Authority through an 'Application for Change.' This application is necessary for substantial modifications, such as:

- Changes in the organization's information.
- Alterations to the completion date.
- Modifications to the project name or area.
- Changes in the number of buildings or project cost.

The fee for this application is **□5,000**, and it must be submitted via the Maha RERA website.

3. Consequences of Non-Compliance

If the Promoter fails to update project details as required, they will receive a notice to comply. Continued non-compliance may result in:

- Suspension of all services provided by RERA.
- Penalties.
- Suspension of the project registration.
- Freezing of the RERA-designated account.

4. Development and Completion Obligations

Section 14 of the Act outlines the obligations of the Promoter regarding project development:

- The Promoter must develop and complete the project per the sanctioned plan, layout plan, and specifications approved by the competent Authority.
- The Promoter cannot make significant additions or alterations to the sanctioned plans, layout plans, or specifications without prior consent from the allottees. However, minor changes required by the allottees or necessary for architectural reasons can be made if recommended and verified by an authorized architect or engineer.
- Any other alterations or additions to the common areas' sanctioned plans, layout plans, or specifications must receive written consent from at least two-thirds of the allottees, excluding the Promoter.

5. Compliance with Amenity Regulations

According to order no. 57/2024 from Maha RERA, all Promoters must provide the exact date of completion for all amenities. This includes detailed specifications about the amenities, such as size, regulations, and permissions. This regulation aims to enhance transparency and boost confidence among home buyers while holding Promoters accountable for their commitments.

Transfer of a Real Estate project

Transfer of a Project to a Third Party

Transferring a real estate project to a third party occurs when the Promoter faces financial difficulties or cannot fulfil project completion requirements due to regulatory issues.

Section 15 of the Act states that:

1. Consent for Transfer:

The Promoter must not transfer or assign the majority of its rights and obligations concerning a real estate project to a third party without getting prior written consent from at least two-thirds of the allottees, excluding the Promoter, and prior written approval from the Authority.

Provision: Such a transfer or assignment shall not affect the allotment of apartments, plots, or buildings made by the original Promoter.

2. Compliance Obligations:

Once the transfer or assignment is approved by the allottees and the Authority as per sub-section (1), the new Promoter is obliged to independently meet all outstanding obligations under the Act and any rules or regulations derived from it, as well as any commitments outlined in the sale agreements made by the previous Promoter with the allottees.

Provision: Importantly, any transfer or assignment approved under this section shall not extend the time frame for the new Promoter to complete the real estate project. The new Promoter remains accountable for fulfilling the previous Promoter's obligations and shall face repercussions for any default in compliance, as delineated by the Act or relevant regulations.

3. Transfer of Title of a Real Estate Project

Section 17 mandates that the Promoter transfer the property title as stipulated in the sale agreement or as mutually agreed upon by the parties involved. In instances where no specific date is mentioned, this transfer must occur within three months of the occupation or completion certificate issuance. Additionally, Rule No. 9 of the Maharashtra Real Estate Rules, 2017, delineates the timeframes and methods for executing the title transfer and addresses situations where the Promoter fails to fulfil their obligations under Section 17, enabling the Authority to mandate the transfer of title. Rule 9(4) outlines the procedure for unilateral deemed conveyance in cases of continued non-compliance.

Chapter 3

Conveyance under RERA

Section 17 of the Act states that:

Execution of Conveyance: The Promoter must complete a registered conveyance deed in favour of the allottee, incorporating proportional undivided ownership in the common areas to the association of allottees of the project or the competent Authority, as relevant. The Promoter must also hand over physical possession of the plot, apartment, or building to the allottees, along with the common areas, to the association or competent Authority, per the specified timeframe outlined in the sanctioned plans under local laws.

Provision: In the absence of any local legislation, the conveyance deed must be executed by the Promoter within three months from the issuance of the occupancy certificate.

Rule 9 of Maha RERA states that:

Formation of Legal Entities: To facilitate the formation of legal entities such as Cooperative Societies, Companies, Associations, and Federations under clause (e) of sub-section (4) of Section 11 of the Act:

(i) If a Cooperative Housing Society or other legal entity for allottees is to be constituted for a single building (not part of a layout) or multiple buildings within a design, the Promoter must submit an application to the Registrar for registration under the Maharashtra Cooperative Societies Act, 1960, within three months of when fifty-one per cent of the total number of allottees have booked their apartments.

(ii) When the Promoter is required to establish an Apex Body as a federation or holding company of separate and independent Cooperative Housing Societies or Companies, they must apply for registration to the Registrar within three months of receiving the occupancy certificate for the last building constructed in the layout.

(iii) Should the Promoter fail to create the legal entity, the Authority may issue an order directing the Promoter to apply to form such an entity, or they may authorize the allottees to proceed with the application.

Remedies for Obtaining Deemed Conveyance

1. **Filing a Criminal Case:** As per Section 13 of the Maharashtra Ownership Flat Act, 1963.
2. **Complaints:** Complaining to the RERA authority.
3. **Consumer Protection Claims:** Initiating a case for defective service under the Consumer Protection Act, 2019.
4. **Application Filing:** Applying to the Authority appointed under Section 5 of the Maharashtra Ownership Flat Act, 1963.

Documents Required for Filing Deemed Conveyance Under MOFA

For Online Application:

- An application in Form 7 for deemed conveyance.
- A certified copy of the 7/12 extract of the property.
- A list of all legal owners of the flat in the society.
- A copy of the Cooperative Housing Society Registration.
- A resolution was passed for deemed conveyance during the general body meeting of the society.
- A legal notice was issued to the Promoter by the society under the Maharashtra Apartment Ownership Act of 1970.
- A copy of the Occupation and Commencement Certificate and one of the approved building plans.
- Court fee stamp of ⊡2,000 or the online fee.
- A self-declaration confirming the accuracy of the applicant's documents.

For Offline Application:

- An application in Form 7 for deemed conveyance.

- A copy of the sale agreement for the flat from one member of the society.
- A copy of Form 7 with the deemed conveyance number.
- A copy of the final approved plan sanctioned by the competent Authority.

Rule 9(3): If the Promoter fails to convey the title as outlined in sub-rule (2) of Rule 9 to the Cooperative Society, Company, Association, or Federation, the Authority shall direct the Promoter to convey the title to the appropriate legal entity.

Rule 9(4): The aforementioned legal entity shall also have the right to execute a unilateral deemed conveyance in its favour and be registered under the Maharashtra Ownership Flats (Regulation of the Promotion of Construction, Sale, Management and Transfer) Act, 1963.

Provisions: Following the conveyance of title to the association of allottees under Section 17, the Promoter retains the right to market, advertise, sell, or offer any unsold apartments, buildings, or plots without restriction. They are also permitted entry to the building premises and common areas to fulfil obligations under sub-section (3) of Section 14.

Furthermore, in cases where development permissions are subject to specific local laws such as the Maharashtra Slum Areas Act, 1971, the Maharashtra Housing and Area Development Authority Act, 1976, the Mumbai Metropolitan Region Development Authority Act, 1974, and others, the title conveyance will be executed by the relevant public Authority within the timeframe stipulated under the applicable law or associated rules and regulations.

Rule 9(5): Upon receipt of the real estate project registration certificate from the Authority, the Promoter must secure insurance as mandated by the Act and other matters notified by the State Government under Section 16 and subsequently hand over the relevant documents to the association, society, federation, or body corporate along with the title conveyance.

De-registration of a project

For instance, when the Promoter wants to file for de-registration, for matters when the project has legal issues, the project is not viable or when the Promoter is unable to complete the project. After getting consent from two-thirds of the allottees, the Promoter must apply for de-registration. The Promoter must provide the allottees a full refund and compensation. A hearing would be conducted for the same by the Authority, and a decision would be made.

On November 12, Maha RERA released a list of 19 real estate projects across Maharashtra for which deregistration has been sought by prominent developers. These projects span cities such as Mumbai, Thane, Pune, Nashik, Nagpur, Kolhapur, and Daman.

Among the projects listed, seven are from Pune district, while Thane accounts for three projects developed by Lodha Group (Macrotech Developers and Palava Dwellers Private Limited). K Raheja Corp has also sought deregistration for three projects in Pune. In Mumbai, Lokhandwala Infrastructure has applied to deregister one project located in Lower Parel.

Other cities, including Nashik, Nagpur, Kolhapur, and Daman, have one project each on the list.

Parking under Maha RERA

Section 2 of the Act defines 'parking' as a part of a common area.

Section 4 of the Act states that the Promoter is entitled to disclose all the detailed information about a parking space in the application for registering a project. The details regarding the number of parking spaces and the allocation must be mentioned clearly in the project plans and documents provided by the Promoter. The buyers must have all the information at the time of receiving the sale agreement. This ensures transparency and prevents the Promoter from misusing and selling open parking spaces to the allottees.

RERA states that open parking is part of the project's common area, and the developer cannot allow it to the allottees. The Promoter is required to execute a conveyance deed in favour of the Association of

Allottees, and the association may then decide to allot the open parking spaces as per the society's bylaws.

Regarding covered, stilt and mechanised parking, the Promoter is eligible to charge the homebuyer for the expenses of constructing such parking spaces.

All these parking spaces are allotted by the Association of Allottees only and not by the Promoter.

Garages can be sold separately to the homebuyers as these spaces come under FSI.

Chapter 4

Gradation of Real Estate Projects

Section 32(f) of the Act emphasises the importance of a grading system for real estate projects and promoters based on various parameters. This initiative aims to enable homebuyers, even those who may not comprehend technical details such as approvals, to assess the quality of a project and make well-informed decisions. By implementing the Grading system, Maha RERA seeks to enhance transparency and facilitate easier understanding of project details for homebuyers.

By seeking public feedback, Maha RERA aims to reline and develop a comprehensive framework that aligns with the needs and expectations of the real estate industry and homebuyers alike. Homebuyers often invest a significant portion of their lifetime savings into buying a home, so they must be aware of the risks involved. Real estate projects can vary significantly in quality, location, and amenities. By grading projects, homebuyers can better understand which projects are the best fit for their needs and budget. By considering the factors included in a grading, home buyers can make more informed decisions about whether or not to invest in a particular project. This system would assess projects based on various factors, including the project's financial viability, Technical Approvals by Competent Authority, and ongoing Legal. Litigations, Promoters Track Record on Compliance in the Project and so on.

Some Risks that Real Estate Grading need to highlight are -

1. Financial Risk
2. Legal Risk
3. Technical Risk
4. Timely Completion Risk

It is important to note that a real estate project's grading does not guarantee that there will be no problems with the project. However, a high grade can give home buyers peace of mind and make them more confident in their investments.

In the first instance, Maha RERA would grade Projects rather than developers. As the system stabilises, the Authority would consider using a matrix to grade promoters as well.

Maha RERA is proposed to adopt the system in the two following phases

Phase 1: Information Disclosure Phase

This would focus on objectively listing all project information. This information would include the following –

1. Project's details:

Location, developer, amenities, and other relevant details

2. Technical Details:

The status of Various Approvals, such as the Commencement Certificate, Promoter Quarterly and annual Compliances, Booking Percentage, and the Status of the Formation of the Society, etc.

3. Financial Details:

Financial Encumbrances, Financial Progress of Projects, Annual Audit Certificate etc.

4. Legal Details:

Litigations & Complaints against this project, Warrants issued, Legal Encumbrances etc.

Phase 2: Project Grading Phase

Eventually, it is proposed to introduce a grading system to rate the projects and, subsequently, promoters based on the above-mentioned and other suitable & relevant criteria.

The phased approach to grading would allow the real estate sector to mature and develop before grades are assigned. This would ensure a fair and accurate grading system and provide a valuable resource for potential buyers.

All Projects registered in January 2023 shall be eligible for Grading of Projects.

Grading can enhance a promoter's reputation, leading to increased marketability and trust. It also helps the authorities monitor and ensure that projects are being developed according to standards, thus improving the overall health of the real estate sector.

The grading shall be automatically generated through Maha RERA's IT Solution MahacRITI on the basis of information submitted by the Promoter. This grading system was introduced by circular no. 46/2023 on 28th August 2023 by Maha RERA.

Chapter 5

Redevelopment under RERA

1. Section 3: Applicability of RERA

Section 3 of RERA establishes the scope of the Act, defining which projects fall under its jurisdiction. This section is crucial as it explicitly includes redevelopment projects among the real estate developments that RERA aims to regulate.

- Inclusion of Redevelopment: Since redevelopment involves demolishing old structures to construct new ones, it falls under the purview of RERA. This inclusion is significant for ensuring that all projects—regardless of their status as new developments or redevelopments—are held to the same standards of transparency, accountability, and consumer protection.
- The rationale behind including redevelopment in RERA is to address the challenges the concerned homebuyers face in such projects, including delays, lack of transparency, and developer accountability. By bringing redevelopment projects under RERA, the Act aims to protect the rights of homebuyers and ensure that developers adhere to the agreed timelines and quality standards.

2. Section 4: Registration of a Redevelopment Project

Section 4 outlines the requirements for developers to register their projects with the regulatory Authority (Maha RERA) before they can market or sell any units within those projects, including redevelopment projects.

- Mandatory Registration: Developers must obtain registration for their redevelopment projects with the Regulatory Authority.
- Regulatory Oversight: Once registered, the project is subject to oversight by Maha RERA, which can monitor compliance with regulations and address any grievances from homebuyers.

In cases of self-redevelopment, where individual flat owners or cooperative housing societies take the initiative to redevelop their own buildings, registration under RERA is not required. This exemption applies because the project is not being marketed or sold to external buyers; rather, it is solely for the benefit of the society's existing members.

- No Registration for Non-Selling Builders: Similarly, if a builder is redeveloping a building solely for its members and does not intend to sell any units to external buyers, RERA registration is not mandated. This allows for greater flexibility for resident-led redevelopment initiatives and private arrangements among members.

Documents to Be Submitted by Promoter for Redevelopment Projects, as per order no. 28/2021

1. Resolution/NOC from Society or Association of Residents (Rehabilitation Component):

A resolution or No Objection Certificate (NOC) from the society or association of residents related to the rehabilitation component. This document must confirm the promoter's right to undertake the redevelopment project.

2. LOI/NOC/Equivalent Document from Planning Authority:

A Letter of Intent (LOI), NOC, or an equivalent document issued by the planning authority. It must confirm the promoter's right to undertake the redevelopment project.

3. Valid Commencement Certificate (Sale Component):

A valid commencement certificate for the sale component of the project, issued by the concerned planning authority.

4. Documents Confirming Promoter Entity's Rights:

All above documents should be in the name of the promoter entity. If the promoter's name is not mentioned in the commencement certificate, any one of the following documents must be submitted to confirm the promoter's right to execute the agreement for sale or other documents:

- Collaboration Agreement
- Development Agreement

- Joint Development Agreement
- Any other form of agreement establishing the rights of the promoter entity.

The submission of these documents ensures the completeness of the registration application. This requirement removes ambiguities regarding the promoter's rights in redevelopment projects.

Part 4
Professional's Corner

Chapter 1

Real Estate Agent

Section 2 (zm) of the Act states that

A real estate agent refers to any individual who, in a professional capacity, facilitates or negotiates on behalf of one party in a transaction involving the sale or transfer of their plot, apartment, or building within a real estate project to another party. This definition also encompasses scenarios where the agent acts on behalf of any other person to transfer their plot, apartment, or building to another individual. The agent receives compensation for their services, including remuneration, fees, commission, or other charges. This definition extends to individuals who, through any medium, introduce potential buyers and sellers to each other to negotiate the sale or purchase of plots, apartments, or buildings. It encompasses property dealers, brokers, and intermediaries, regardless of the title they are referred to, such as brokers, middlemen, or any other designation.

Registration of a Real Estate Agent

Section 9 of the Act states that

No real estate agent shall facilitate the sale or purchase of or act on behalf of any person to facilitate the sale or purchase of any plot, apartment or building, as the case may be, in a real estate project or part of it, without obtaining registration under this section.

Every real estate agent shall make an application to the Authority for registration in such form and manner, within such time, and accompanied by such fee and documents as may be prescribed.

Rule 11 of Maha RERA states that –

Mandatory Registration: Every real estate agent required to be registered under sub-section (2) of section 9 must submit an application in writing for registered real estate projects. This application should be made immediately and, in any case, before engaging in any activities related to the marketing, advertising, sale, or purchase of any apartments.

Application Requirements: It must be submitted in Form 'G' and accompanied by the following documents:

1. **Enterprise Details:** Brief information about the enterprise the agent is associated with, including its name, registered business address, type of enterprise (proprietorship firm, society, partnership, company, etc.), registration numbers, PAN, Aadhaar Card No., DIN, and any other relevant registration under which statutory returns are required to be filed.
2. **Legal Registrations:** Details of any registrations obtained under other laws, along with copies of authenticated documents such as partnership deeds, memorandum of association, articles of association, etc.
3. **Photographs:** Recent colour photographs of the real estate agent (if the agent is an individual) and of all partners, directors, trustees, etc., including individuals in service or involved in activities expected of a real estate agent in the case of other entities.
4. **Income-Tax Returns:** Income-tax returns for the last three financial years preceding the application. If the applicant was exempted from filing returns during any of the three years, a declaration to this effect should be provided.
5. **Business Address Proof:** Authenticated proof of address of the principal place of business, along with the contact details (including telephone numbers, fax numbers, and email addresses) of any branch offices.
6. **Project Details:** Information on all real estate projects and their promoters for whom the agent has acted in the preceding five years.
7. **Pending Cases:** Details of any civil or criminal cases pending against the agent (if an individual) or against any of the partners, directors, trustees, etc., in the case of other entities.

8. **Document Samples:** Authenticated copies of all letterheads, rubber stamp images, and acknowledgement receipts proposed for use by the real estate agent.
9. **Additional Information:** Any other information and documents as may be specified by regulations.

   Registration Fees:

- A fee of ₹10,000 for individual applicants.
- A fee of ₹1,00,000 for applicants other than individuals.

  The registration fees must be paid through NEFT, RTGS, or any other approved digital transaction mode.

10. **Maintenance of Records:** Once a promoter engages a real estate agent under clause (f) of sub-section (2) of section 4 for a real estate project, the real estate agent is required to maintain and preserve separate books of account, records, and documents for each project.
11. **Validity and Renewal of Registration:** A real estate agent's registration is valid for five years from the date of registration. After the expiration of the five years, the registration must be renewed.

The application for renewal and the requisite renewal fees should be submitted at least sixty days before the registration expires.

Section 9 and Rule 12 of Maha RERA states that

Authority's Role in Registration: The Authority is responsible for granting or rejecting the registration of real estate agents within a prescribed time frame and manner. This process includes verifying that all conditions stipulated by the Act and rules and regulations are met. The actions taken by the Authority are as follows:

(a) **Grant of Registration:** Upon fulfilment of all prescribed conditions, the Authority will grant a single registration to the real estate agent, applicable across the entire State or Union Territory, as the case may be.

(b) **Rejection of Application:** If the application does not conform to the provisions of the Act, rules, or regulations, the Authority may reject it. The reasons for rejection need to be recorded in writing.

Opportunity to be Heard: No application shall be rejected without first providing the applicant with an opportunity to present their case. This ensures that the applicant's rights to a fair hearing are upheld.

Deemed Registration: If the Authority does not communicate any deficiencies or rejection of the application within the specified period as per sub-section (3), the applicant is deemed to have been registered. This provision prevents unnecessary delays in the registration process and provides clarity and assurance to the applicant regarding their registration status.

Issuance of Registration Number: Once registered under the Act, every real estate agent is issued a unique registration number by the Authority. The agent must quote this number in every sale facilitated under this Act. This requirement ensures transparency and accountability in real estate transactions.

Revocation or Suspension of Registration: The Authority may suspend or revoke the existing registration of a real estate agent in the following circumstances:

- **Violation of Conditions:** If the real estate agent violates any of the conditions of their registration or any terms and conditions specified under the Act, rules, or regulations.
- **Misrepresentation or Fraud:** If the registration was obtained through misrepresentation or fraud, the Authority has the right to revoke or suspend it.

The duration of the suspension is at the Authority's discretion, based on the severity of the breach or violation.

Opportunity to be Heard: Before revocation or suspension, the real estate agent must be allowed to be heard. This procedural safeguard ensures that decisions are made fairly and that the real estate agent can defend themselves against the allegations.

Rule 13 of Maha RERA – Renewal of Registration for Real Estate Agents

1. **Application for Renewal:** A real estate agent registered under Section 9 of the Act may apply to renew their existing registration at least sixty days before its expiry. The application for renewal must be submitted in the prescribed format and accompanied by the same fees as applicable for new registrations under these rules.
2. **Documents for Renewal:** The agent must submit updated documents specified in Rule 11 and the renewal application. The Authority shall communicate the decision regarding the renewal to the real estate agent in Form 'K'. In case of rejection, the agent will be informed through Form 'T'.
3. Provided that no renewal application shall be rejected unless the applicant has been allowed to present their case.
4. **Grant of Renewal:** The registration renewal shall be granted if the real estate agent continues to adhere to the provisions of the Act and the rules and regulations made thereunder.
5. **Validity of Renewed Registration:** Upon approval, the renewed registration will be valid for five more years from the date of renewal. The registration is initially granted for five years, and it can be renewed thereafter by paying the prescribed renewal fee.

Functions and Obligations of a Real Estate Agent

Every registered agent is obligated to:

(a) **Prohibition on Facilitating Unregistered Sales:** Avoid facilitating the sale of any building, plot, or apartment in a real estate project or any part thereof sold by the promoter in any planning area if the project is not registered with the Authority.

(b) **Maintenance of Records:** Maintain and preserve such books of records and accounts as may be prescribed.

(c) **Avoidance of Unfair Trade Practices:** Refrain from engaging in unfair trade practices, including but not limited to:

Making any statement, whether orally, in writing, or through visible representation, which:

i. Misleads representation of services

ii. **False Affiliations:** Claims that the promoter or the agent has approval or affiliation that they do not possess.

iii. **Deceptive Information:** Provides false or misleading information concerning the services offered.

iv. **Misleading Advertisements:** This law allows the publication of advertisements in any medium, including newspapers, for services that are not intended to be offered.

(d) **Provision of Information:** Ensure that all information and documents that the allottee is entitled to receive at the time of booking any plot, apartment, or building are made available.

(e) **Other Prescribed Functions:** Perform such other duties and functions as may be prescribed by the regulations.

(f) **Display and Usage of Registration Number:** Every registered real estate agent must prominently display the registration certificate number at their principal place of business and branch offices. The registration number must also be quoted on all documents related to advertisement, marketing, selling, or purchasing activities, along with the registration certificate number of the real estate project.

Rule 17 of Maha RERA – Responsibilities of Real Estate Agents

Real estate agents are expected to assist the allottee and the promoter in exercising their respective rights and fulfilling their obligations during the marketing, selling, purchase, and sale of any plot, apartment, or building, as the case may be. They must not engage in any unfair trade practices, including:

1. Misrepresentation of Services:

Making any statement, whether orally, in writing, or through visible representation, that:

- **False Service Standards**
- **Unfounded Affiliations:** Claims of approval or affiliation that the promoter or agent does not possess.
- **Misleading Service Information:** Provides false or misleading information about services offered by the promoter.

2. False Advertisements: Allowing the publication of advertisements in any medium, including newspapers, for services not intended to be offered by the promoter.

3. Provision of Information to Allottee: Ensuring that the allottee has access to all relevant information and documents when booking a plot, apartment, or building.

4. Compliance with Regulations: Performing such other functions as prescribed by the Authority's regulations.

These rules and obligations aim to establish a transparent and fair environment in the real estate market, promote the interests of all stakeholders, and ensure compliance with the regulatory framework.

Impact of RERA on Real Estate Agents

The changes that RERA has put forth for Agents are as follows –

Registration Requirement

As per Section 9 of the RERA Act, all real estate agents must register with the RERA authority in their respective states. They cannot engage in any real estate transactions without this registration. Agents are issued a unique registration number that must be quoted in all transactions.

Adherence to the Code of Conduct

Honesty and Transparency:

Section 10 mandates that agents act transparently in all their dealings, providing accurate information regarding properties.

No Misleading Information:

As stipulated under this section, agents are prohibited from providing false information that may mislead clients. Violation would lead to penalties, including suspension or cancellation of registration.

Role in Ensuring Compliance

Promoting Registered Projects:

Under Sections 9 and 10, agents can only deal in projects registered with RERA.

Informing Buyers:

They must inform buyers of all relevant details about a project, including its legal status, approvals, and progress.

No Engagement with Unregistered Developers:

Agents must avoid dealing with developers who are not registered under RERA.

Maintenance of Records

Documentation:

Agents must maintain a detailed book of records of all transactions and communications, as required under Section 10.

Transaction Records:

These records should be available for audits or inspections by RERA authorities.

Fiduciary Responsibilities

Act in the Best Interest of the Client:

Section 10 emphasises that agents must act in the best interest of their clients and provide them with the best possible advice.

Avoid Conflict of Interest:

The section also mandates that agents avoid conflict of interest in their transactions.

Penalties and Legal Compliance

Penalties for Non-Compliance:

Section 9 outlines penalties for agents who do not comply with RERA regulations, including fines, suspension, or cancellation of their registration. An Agent would be fined Rs. 10,000 for every day they operate without a registration, and the cumulative fine can reach 5% of the cost of the property for which the transaction was facilitated. The fines follow a similar pattern for other non-compliances by agents. If an agent continues to violate the provisions of RERA, he could even be imprisoned for a year or maybe fined up to 10% of the cost of the property.

Legal Obligations:

Agents must ensure compliance with all legal obligations under RERA, including proper documentation and adherence to financial guidelines.

Assistance in Dispute Resolution

Facilitating Dispute Resolution:

Under Section 31, agents may help resolve disputes between buyers and developers, especially if the dispute involves their conduct.

Disclosure of Commission

Transparency in Commission:

Section 10 requires agents to disclose their commission structure and any financial arrangements related to the transaction to all parties involved.

RERA examination and Certification

A. Purpose of RERA Examination and Certification

The RERA certification aims to:

Ensure that all real estate agents have a uniform understanding of the laws, rules, and regulations governing real estate transactions under RERA, promote ethical practices and professionalism among agents and ensure that consumers are dealing with certified professionals who can provide accurate information and advice.

B. Who Needs to Take the RERA Examination?

Individuals who wish to become real estate agents after the implementation of RERA must pass the certification exam before they can be registered under RERA.

Some states may require existing agents to pass the exam to continue their registration under RERA. Eg: Maha RERA.

C. RERA Examination Syllabus

The syllabus for the RERA exam generally covers the following topics:

- Detailed provisions, objectives, and implications of the Act.
- Legal aspects of buying, selling, and leasing properties.
- Procedures for registering real estate projects and agents under RERA.
- Ethical practices, code of conduct, and fiduciary responsibilities.
- Rights of buyers and sellers under RERA.
- Understanding the mechanisms provided by RERA for resolving disputes.
- Guidelines on financial transactions, including the use of escrow accounts and fee disclosures.
- State-specific modifications and rules under RERA.

D. RERA Examination Process

i. Application for Examination

The agents must meet the eligibility criteria set by the respective state's RERA authority (e.g., minimum educational qualifications, age, etc. They must apply for the exam through the official Maha RERA website. They may need to provide personal details, educational qualifications, and work experience. An application fee is usually required, varying from state to state.

ii. Examination Structure

The exam is conducted online and typically consists of multiple-choice questions (MCQs). It may last 1 to 3 hours, and candidates must achieve a minimum passing percentage of 50% to be certified.

iii. Study Material and Preparation

Maha RERA provides a detailed syllabus and recommends study resources, such as online seminars and courses on RERA that may educate one on the various aspects of the Act. Mock Test are provided by both Maha RERA and third parties to aid agents in clearing the examination.

iv. Examination Day

Candidates must present valid ID proof, such as a PAN or AADHAAR. The examination is supervised by invigilators to ensure utmost honesty.

E. Certification Process

After passing the examination, the agent is issued a certification, allowing them to apply for registration with Maha RERA.

The certification is valid for a limited period, after which renewal is required.

The agents are encouraged to participate in ongoing education programs to stay up to date with the changes in Real Estate Laws.

F. Self-Regulatory Organisations

Section 32 of the Act allows for forming SROs for Real Estate Agents in Maharashtra. These organisations help standardise practices, set ethical standards, and ensure agents operate within a certain regulatory framework. They also provide platforms for resolving disputes and addressing grievances between agents, clients and developers, thus reducing the burden on Maha RERA.

They also play a crucial role in the ongoing training and development of agents, offering workshops, seminars, and courses that help agents stay up to date about the market's trends.

G. Financial Guidelines

Section 10 emphasises the importance of transparency in all financial transactions agents conduct. They must ensure that all these transactions are properly documented.

Maha RERA mandates that funds be placed in an escrow account for certain transactions. This ensures that the money is solely used for its purpose and provides an additional layer of protection for the buyers.

Agents are even prohibited from accepting advance payments from buyers without a formal agreement in place. They are also required to disclose the fee (commission) amount upfront, ensuring that the buyers are fully aware of the costs involved in the transaction from the outset.

Chapter 2

Architect under RERA

Section 2(h) of the RERA Act states that –

An "architect" means any person registered as an architect, under the provisions of the Architects Act, 1972.

Architects are governed by the governing body viz. Council of Architecture (COA), which was constituted by the Government of India under provisions of Architects Act, 1972. The Council of Architecture is responsible to regulate the education and practice of architecture India besides maintaining the register of architects.

Roles and responsibilities of an Architect

1. To issue a regular certificate in Form 1 about the percentage of completion of the project to the promoter to facilitate the withdrawal of the amount from the RERA Designated Bank Account.
2. To issue a certificate in Form 4 after the project is completed as per the occupation certificate issued by the competent Authority.
3. To prepare the layout of the project layout and buildings as per the requirements of the client, within the development regulations.
4. To submit proposals of project layouts, carpet area and buildings plans to the civic/planning authority for its approval and also to obtain development permission (commencement certificate) for the building/s.
5. To create 3D renderings and models for marketing.
6. To provide all necessary documents to the contractor.
7. To ensure that the construction is being done within all permitted guidelines.
8. To ensure all necessary approvals are obtained.

9. To obtain the completion and occupancy certificates after the completion of construction.
10. To handle all necessary documents for the promoter and ensure they are submitted and filed on time and to the relevant authorities.

Form 1 under RERA

Form 1 under RERA is primarily handled by the architect who is involved in the project. The architect plays a crucial part in ensuring that all necessary details are accurately provided, certifying the progress of the project, and updating the RERA authority regularly.

1. Project Information:

- Project Name: The architect must provide the name of the project.
- Location Details: The exact location of the project, including boundaries, plot numbers, and survey numbers, must be furnished by the architect.
- Commencement and Completion Dates: The architect certifies and submits the start and end dates of the project construction.

2. Architect's Credentials:

- Name and Contact Details: The architect provides their personal and professional details, including registration number and contact information.
- Professional Responsibility: The architect acknowledges their role in certifying the project and vouches for the authenticity of the information provided.

3. Legal Title Report

- The architect ensures that a legal title report is attached, confirming the land ownership or development rights, and certifies that the land is free from encumbrances, if applicable.

4. Sanctions and Approvals:

- The architect must ensure that copies of all government-approved plans and permissions, including building plan

approvals, environmental clearances (if applicable), and layout plan approvals, are submitted.
- Ongoing compliance with all statutory regulations is confirmed by the architect through certification.

5. Construction Progress Certification:

- The architect certifies the progress of the construction work, confirming that it is in line with the approved plans and specifications.
- The architect is responsible for providing periodic updates (quarterly or as required) on the status of construction, including milestones achieved.

6. Architect's Declaration:

- The architect provides an affidavit stating that they have overseen the design and construction work, ensuring that it complies with all statutory norms and guidelines.
- The architect certifies that the project is being developed in accordance with the RERA regulations, approved layout plans, and relevant approvals.
- Undertaking that there will be no deviation from the sanctioned plans without prior approval.

7. Financial Progress:

- The architect ensures that financial aspects related to construction progress are tracked, certifying that funds are being utilized for the construction and land cost as per RERA guidelines.

8. Other Disclosures:

- The architect certifies any ongoing litigation, encumbrances, or mortgages related to the project.
- Any modification to the project after registration requires the architect's certification and approval.

Form 4 under RERA

Form 4 under RERA is filed by the architect who plays a critical role in certifying the completion of a real estate project. The architect is responsible for ensuring that the project adheres to the approved plans, providing necessary certifications at various stages of completion, and ultimately submitting the Completion Certificate to the RERA authority.

1. Completion of Construction:

- The architect certifies that the real estate project has been completed as per the approved plans, layout, structural designs, and other specifications.
- The architect verifies and confirms that all construction work, including any changes or modifications, complies with the sanctioned plans and has followed RERA guidelines.

2. Filing of Form 4:

- The architect is responsible for filling out and submitting Form 4 to the respective RERA authority upon completion of the project.
- The architect ensures that all the required information is accurate and up to date, including details of the project, completion date, and adherence to all statutory approvals.

3. Certificates Issued by the Architect:

- Completion Certificate:
- The architect issues the Completion Certificate, confirming that the project has been completed as per the approved plans and specifications.
- This certificate ensures that the constructed building is safe to be occupied and that all regulatory requirements have been fulfilled.
- Occupancy Certificate:
- The architect collaborates with other professionals (if required) to ensure that the Occupancy Certificate is issued, allowing the project to be legally occupied.
- It confirms that all essential infrastructure (water, electricity, fire safety, etc.) is in place and functioning properly.

4. Adherence to Approved Plans:

- The architect certifies that there have been no deviations from the approved building plans or layout unless prior permission was obtained from the RERA authority.

- If any alterations or modifications were made, the architect ensures that these changes were sanctioned by the competent authorities.

5. Compliance with Statutory Approvals:

- The architect verifies that all necessary statutory approvals (building plan approval, environmental clearance, safety measures, etc.) have been followed throughout the construction process.
- This includes compliance with fire safety norms, structural safety standards, and other applicable legal requirements.

6. Progress Certificates During Construction:

- The architect is responsible for submitting progress certificates at various stages of construction (as required) before the final completion. These certificates ensure that the project is progressing as per the approved plans.
- At each stage, the architect confirms that construction quality and standards are being met.

7. Architect's Declaration:

- The architect provides a declaration in Form 4 that they have personally overseen the construction and certify its completion as per the approved plans.
- The declaration includes an assurance that the building is fit for occupancy, all safety standards have been met, and that the architect bears responsibility for the accuracy of the information provided.

8. Submission of Related Documents:

- The architect attaches all necessary documents with Form 4, including:
- Project layout and building plans.
- Statutory approvals.
- Photographs of the completed project.
- Structural stability certificate (if required).
- These documents support the architect's claim that the project is completed as per the sanctioned plans.

Chapter 3

Civil Engineer under RERA

A civil engineer is a professional who oversees construction projects. They are the ones responsible for the complete construction, functionality and safety of the project.

Section 2(u) of the act states that

"engineer" means a person who possesses a bachelor's degree or equivalent from an institution recognised by the All-India Council of Technical Education University or recognised Institution.

Roles and responsibilities of a Civil Engineer

Here are the concise roles and responsibilities of a civil engineer under RERA:

1. Ensure construction follows approved plans and specifications.
2. Monitor construction progress and provide regular updates.
3. Ensure structural integrity and compliance with safety standards.
4. Supervise daily construction activities and site safety.
5. Certify completion of construction stages and issue necessary certificates.
6. Assist in budget estimation and cost control.
7. Maintain compliance documentation and submit reports to RERA.
8. Ensure proper utilization of project funds as per RERA guidelines.
9. Collaborate with architects, contractors, and promoters for smooth project execution.

Form 2 under RERA

Form 2 under the RERA act is handled by the civil engineer, who plays a key role in certifying the structural safety and progress of the project. The civil engineer is responsible for submitting Form 2, ensuring that the project's construction aligns with approved designs, safety standards, and quality benchmarks.

1. Filing of Form 2

- The civil engineer is responsible for completing and filing Form 2 with the RERA authority.
- The form certifies that the project is being constructed according to approved structural plans and standards.

2. Structural Safety Certification:

- The civil engineer certifies that the structure is designed and constructed to hold the required loads and stresses, adhering to safety norms.
- The engineer verifies the strength and stability of the building, ensuring compliance with relevant codes and regulations.

3. Quality Assurance:

- The civil engineer ensures that all materials used meet the approved specifications.
- They certify that the construction quality is up to the standards outlined in the project approval.

4. Construction Progress Certification:

- The civil engineer provides stage-wise certifications, confirming the completion of specific construction phases.
- These certifications are required for the promoter to withdraw funds from the project's escrow account.

5. Supervision and Compliance:

- The civil engineer supervises construction work, ensuring compliance with the approved plans, structural design, and safety guidelines.

- They certify that there have been no unauthorized changes or deviations from the approved plans.

6. **Verification of Load-bearing Capacity:**
   - The civil engineer certifies the foundation and structural elements of the building, ensuring they meet load-bearing requirements.
   - This includes certifying that soil testing and other geotechnical evaluations have been appropriately considered in the design.
7. **Material Testing and Certification:**
   - The civil engineer conducts and certifies the results of material testing (concrete, steel, etc.) to ensure that they meet the required quality standards.
   - They provide documentation verifying the safety and integrity of construction materials used.
8. **Role in Issuance of Completion Certificates:**
   - The civil engineer collaborates with other professionals to ensure that the Completion Certificate is issued upon the project's finalization, confirming that construction complies with RERA standards.
   - Their certification is vital for obtaining occupancy rights.
9. **Final Declaration:**
   - The civil engineer provides a final declaration in Form 2 stating that they have reviewed and supervised the construction, and it meets all safety, structural, and regulatory requirements.

Quality Assurance Certificate

A Quality Assurance Certificate is an official document provided by a qualified civil engineer, that certifies the quality of construction, the materials used, and adherence to design standards. Under the RERA Act this certificate ensures that the construction of a real estate project complies with approved plans, industry standards, and relevant safety guidelines.

The Quality Assurance Certificate serves as a formal confirmation that the project meets all necessary quality standards, and it is issued after thorough inspection and testing at various stages of the construction process.

Why is a Quality Assurance Certificate Needed?

1. Ensuring Construction Quality:

- The primary purpose of the certificate is to ensure that the materials used (e.g., cement, steel, bricks) and the construction techniques comply with the specifications approved by authorities. This helps maintain high construction quality and prevents the use of substandard materials that could compromise the structural integrity of the building.

2. Compliance with RERA Regulations:

- Under RERA, promoters are required to adhere to certain standards for construction quality, safety, and timelines. The Quality Assurance Certificate ensures compliance with these regulations and acts as proof that the project is being developed according to approved plans and legal norms.

3. Building Safety and Structural Integrity:

- The certificate ensures that the project is safe for its intended purpose (residential or commercial use). It certifies that the structure has the necessary load-bearing capacity, can withstand environmental stressors (like earthquakes, wind, etc.), and meets all safety regulations.

4. Transparency and Accountability:

- One of the key objectives of RERA is to bring transparency and trust to the sector. By providing a Quality Assurance Certificate, the developer and civil engineer assure buyers that the project is of high quality, safe, and built as per approved standards. This reduces the risk of construction defects, and buyers gain confidence in the project's integrity.

5. Regulatory Approval and Financing:

- Many financial institutions and regulatory bodies require a Quality Assurance Certificate before approving financing for real estate projects. The certificate demonstrates that the project is progressing in compliance with safety and quality standards, making it easier for developers to secure funding.

6. **Escrow Fund Withdrawals:**
   - In RERA-registered projects, developers can only withdraw money from the project's escrow account based on the completion of certain construction stages. The Quality Assurance Certificate is critical at these milestones as it confirms the quality of work done and allows the release of funds from the escrow account to the promoter.
7. **Risk Mitigation for Developers and Buyers:**
   - The certificate helps minimize the risk of future issues related to construction quality, such as structural failure or defects. This protects both the developer from potential legal and financial liability and the buyers from purchasing a property that may need extensive repairs in the future.
8. **Certifying Safety Standards:**
   - A Quality Assurance Certificate ensures that safety protocols, such as fire safety, electrical safety, and plumbing standards, are met. This is crucial for the long-term usability and safety of the building.

Role of the Civil Engineer in Issuing a Quality Assurance Certificate:

1. **Supervision of Construction:**
   - The civil engineer is responsible for the entire construction process to ensure that the work adheres to the approved plans, design standards, and quality norms. They play a hands-on role in inspecting each stage of construction.
2. **Material Testing and Quality Control:**
   - The civil engineer coordinates with testing laboratories to ensure materials like concrete, steel, and bricks meet the required strength and quality standards. They assess the test reports and make sure that only high-quality materials are used.

3. Issuing the Certificate:

- After verifying that all construction standards and specifications are met, the civil engineer issues the Quality Assurance Certificate. This document becomes a part of the project's regulatory and compliance documentation under RERA.

Defect liability under RERA

Section 14(3) of the Act states If the allottee notifies the promoter of any structural or workmanship defects, or any failure to meet obligations under the sale agreement within five years of taking possession, the promoter must rectify the issues within thirty days at no extra cost. If the promoter fails to do so, the aggrieved allottees are entitled to receive suitable compensation as outlined in this Act.

Chapter 4

Chartered Accountant under RERA

A chartered accountant (CA) under RERA ensures financial transparency and compliance by certifying the appropriate use of funds collected from homebuyers, conducting audits, and preparing necessary reports. Their role is crucial in safeguarding stakeholder interests, promoting accountability, and ensuring that real estate projects adhere to regulatory financial guidelines.

Form 3 under RERA

Form 3 under the RERA Act is crucial for monitoring and regulating the financial aspects of real estate projects. The chartered accountant is responsible for filing Form 3, ensuring that the project's financials are transparent, compliant with regulations, and that funds are utilized as per RERA guidelines.

1. Filing of Form 3:

- This form certifies the correct utilization of funds from the project's designated escrow account, ensuring compliance with RERA financial regulations.

2. Certification of Fund Utilization:

- The CA certifies that 70% of the project funds, including amounts received from allottees, are deposited in a separate bank account (escrow account) dedicated to construction and land costs.
- They verify that funds withdrawn from the escrow account are utilized solely for the development and construction of the project, as per RERA norms.

3. Project Cost and Financial Audit:

- The chartered accountant certifies the total cost of the project, including land acquisition costs, construction costs, and all the other related expenditures.

- They conduct a financial audit of the project to ensure that the promoter's claims about the costs and funds utilized are accurate and transparent.

4. **Stage-wise Certification of Funds:**
   - The CA provides stage-wise certification for the withdrawal of funds from the escrow account. Funds can only be withdrawn in proportion to the completion of each stage of the project, as certified by the civil engineer and architect.
   - This ensures that funds are used efficiently and in alignment with project progress.
5. **Ensuring Financial Compliance with RERA:**
   - The CA ensures that the promoter complies with Section 4(2)(l)(D) of the RERA Act, which mandates that funds are utilized solely for the construction and land costs of the project.
   - They ensure that the 70-30 rule is followed, where 70% of the funds are reserved for construction and land costs, and 30% is allowed for other expenses.
6. **Verification of Promoter's Financial Records:**
   - The CA verifies the financial records of the promoter, including receipts from allottees, construction-related expenses, and other project costs.
   - They ensure that no funds are misappropriated or diverted to unrelated projects or personal use by the promoter.
7. **Final Certification for Completion:**
   - Once the project is nearing completion, the CA provides a final certification that the funds have been appropriately utilized in accordance with the project's financial plan.
   - This certification is crucial for the issuance of the Completion Certificate and the project's financial closure under RERA.
8. **Audit of Escrow Account:**
   - The CA is responsible for auditing the escrow account to ensure that all funds deposited and withdrawn comply with RERA regulations.

- They verify that the funds drawn from the escrow account are in proportion to the project's completion as certified by other professionals involved in the project.

9. Role in Ensuring Financial Transparency:

- The chartered accountant ensures financial transparency by verifying that all financial transactions of the project are properly documented and in compliance with all legal requirements.
- Their certification ensures that both buyers and regulatory authorities can trust that the funds are being utilized as intended.

10. Detailed Financial Statements:

- The CA prepares and submits detailed financial statements, including:
- Sources of funding (allottee payments, loans, etc.).
- Expenditure statements for land, construction, and other project-related expenses.
- Bank account statements of the escrow account.
- These statements ensure the financial health and accountability of the project.

Form 5 under RERA

Form 5 under RERA is the Annual Audit Report that must be filed by a chartered accountant at the end of each financial year, certifying the project's financial statements and fund utilization. It ensures compliance with RERA regulations, providing transparency regarding the financial health of the real estate project.

Form 3 vs. Form 5

Aspect	Form 3	Form 5
Purpose	Certifies fund utilization from the escrow account for land and construction costs.	Serves as the Annual Audit Report for the project, detailing overall financial compliance.

Aspect	Form 3	Form 5
Filing Responsibility	Filed by the **chartered accountant** to ensure appropriate fund usage.	Also filed by the **chartered accountant** to certify the financial statements and audit results.
Frequency	Filed as needed, typically at various project stages or milestones.	Filed annually at the end of each financial year.
Focus	Focuses specifically on the **utilization of funds** and compliance with the 70-30 rule.	Focuses on the overall **financial health** of the project, including all income and expenditures.
Detail Level	Provides a snapshot of fund allocation related to specific construction stages.	Offers a comprehensive view of the project's financial records over the year.
Compliance Assurance	Ensures compliance with specific fund utilization regulations.	Ensures overall compliance with RERA's financial regulations and guidelines.
Impact on Project	Affects fund release for ongoing construction.	Influences the overall financial standing and credibility of the project for investors and buyers.

Chapter 5

Advocate under RERA

An advocate is a licensed legal professional who represents clients in legal matters, providing advice, preparing legal documents, and appearing in court on their behalf. They possess specialized knowledge of the law and are responsible for safeguarding the rights and interests of their clients.

Roles and Responsibilities of an Advocate under RERA

1. Legal Representation:

- Advocates represent clients, including developers and homebuyers, in legal proceedings related to real estate disputes under the RERA Act.

2. Advising on Compliance:

- They provide legal advice to developers on compliance with RERA regulations, ensuring that all project documentation meets the necessary legal standards.

3. Drafting and Reviewing Documents:

- Advocates are responsible for drafting and reviewing crucial legal documents, including:
- Title Certificate: Certifies the ownership and the legal status of the property, ensuring there are no encumbrances.
- Allotment Letter: Issued to buyers upon successful application for property, detailing the terms of the allotment.
- Agreement for Sale: A legal contract between the buyer and seller outlining the terms of the property sale, including price, payment terms, and conditions.
- Sale Deed: The final document that transfers ownership from the seller to the buyer, which must be registered as per the law.

4. Resolving Disputes:

- Advocates assist in resolving disputes between developers and homebuyers, including issues related to project delays, fund mismanagement, and violation of agreement terms.

5. Filing Complaints:

- They help clients file complaints with RERA in cases of non-compliance by developers or grievances regarding property transactions.

6. Conducting Due Diligence:

- Advocates conduct due diligence to verify property documents, ensuring that all legal aspects are in order before a transaction is finalized.

7. Mediation and Negotiation:

- They engage in mediation and negotiation between parties to reach amicable settlements without litigation, which can save time and resources.

8. Educating Clients:

- Advocates educate clients about their rights and obligations under RERA, ensuring they understand the legal implications of their transactions.

9. Assisting in Registration:

- They assist clients in the registration process of sale deeds and other relevant documents, ensuring compliance with local regulations and legal requirements.

Advocates play a crucial role in the real estate sector under RERA by ensuring legal compliance, protecting client interests, and facilitating smooth property transactions. Their expertise in drafting essential documents like title certificates, allotment letters, agreements for sale, and sale deeds is vital for safeguarding the rights of all parties involved.

Part 5
RERA as a Judiciary

Chapter 1

Complaint Filing under RERA

The main purpose of the RERA Act of 2016 is to safeguard the Allottees' interests and provide maximum transparency throughout. One way this is done is through the well-defined complaint procedure set up by RERA, which provides quick solutions. The Authority can call for information, conduct investigations (section 35), issue interim orders (section 36), issue directions (section 37), and impose penalties or interest.

As per Section 79, all disputes and complaints related to the real estate project cannot be referred in any civil court and are under the jurisdiction of the Authority, the Adjudicating officer, or the Appellate Tribunal. However, the matter may be taken before the Consumer Dispute Redressal Commission under the Consumer Protection Act 2019, as they are considered the alternative remedy, not the civil Court. Similarly, a group of 10% of the allottees or 100 allottees, whichever is less, may also file the complaint before the National Company Law Tribunal (NCLT) as per the Insolvency and Bankruptcy Code of 2016, as the Code has overriding effect as held by the Hon'ble Supreme Court.

The complaints may be filed by any aggrieved person against any of the involved parties for negligence.

Note: Third parties are not eligible to file a complaint before RERA.

The word 'person' includes the Association of allottees or it could include any Voluntary Consumer Association registered under any law. The complaint may be against the violations of any of the provisions of the Act, Rule and regulations made thereunder. The complaint may be filed against the promoter, allottee or the real estate agent. The complaint is to be made in the form and manner as mentioned under rules 6 and 7 of the Maha RERA Rules, 2017. The applicant or appellant may either appear in person or authorise one or more chartered accountants, company secretaries, accountants, legal practitioners, or any officers to present their case before the Appellate Tribunal, the adjudicating officer, or the Authority under Section 56.

"As per order no. 11/2019, dated 23rd October 2019, of Maha RERA, group complaints, such as those made by an Association of Allottees, shall be entertained only regarding common relief claimed under sections 7 and 8 of RERA. An individual complaint must be filed separately for individual reliefs, as the association cannot file the complaint to claim the relief for any individual."

It is essential to note the following:

- RERA does not guarantee or assure any order/outcome.
- A favourable order does not translate to a guaranteed receipt of money.
- An order passed in favour of the Allottees merely entitles them to receive the money.
- Hearings may be delayed due to the huge pendency of cases.
- The compensation may not be honoured by the respondents.
- RERA is not responsible for any losses or lack of gains arising from an unfavourable order passed by them.
- The order passed in Allottees' favour can be appealed by the respondents.

Complaints could be filed for the following reasons:

- Compensation and interest to the allottees for delay in giving possession. Section 18(1)
- Non-execution of Registered Agreement of sale. Section 13
- Irregular or unilateral cancellation of allotment. Section 11(5)
- Compensation for the defective title of the land, without any time limitation. Section 18(2)
- If the project is not completed within the stipulated time, the money taken from allottees will be refunded along with interest as prescribed in the rules.
- Revocation of Registration for persistent violations made by the promoter and for unfair trade practices. Section 7

- Enforcement of rights of Allottees or to enforce obligations of the promoters towards the allottees. Section 11-19

The promoter may file a complaint against an allottee under the following circumstances:

- If the allottee does not accept the possession of the apartment
- If the allottee does not show cooperation for the formation of a society or an Association of Allottees
- If the allottee does not make the payments as per the terms of the agreement
- If the allottee carries out changes in the apartment which affect the construction of the building
- If the allottee does not carry out his duties as prescribed under RERA or obstructs the promoter or the real estate agent from doing their duties
- If the allottee does not provide the necessary documents when needed
- If the allottee violates any of the terms of the agreement

Manner of filing a complaint

1. Online complaint filing module

The aggrieved person may visit the Maha RERA website and go to the complaint redressal section. There, they must fill in all the details about themselves, the person/entity they are filing the complaint against, and the incident/issue for which the complaint is being filed. They will then get all the details about the hearing on the RERA dashboard itself.

2. Offline complaint filing

The aggrieved person may download the complaint form from the RERA website, fill it out, attach the necessary documents, pay the prescribed fee, and then submit the form and documents to the RERA office.

3. Through an authorized representative

The aggrieved person can hire a professional, such as a CA or an advocate, to file the complaint.

Authorities handling the complaints

1. Maharashtra Real Estate Regulatory Authority (RERA):

RERA handles all complaints other than compensation determinations. Depending on the nature of the complaint, RERA can levy interest or charge a penalty.

2. Adjudicating Officer

RERA in consultation with the government, appoints an Adjudicating officer to handle all complaints relating to loss and damages. The adjudicating officer is eligible to grant the aggrieved person suitable compensation.

Inquiry by the Authority

Rule 6(2) of Maha RERA states that -

Upon receiving the complaint, the Authority will send a notice to the respondent containing details of the alleged violation and relevant documents. The notice will include a specific date and time for a subsequent hearing. On the scheduled date, the Authority will inform the respondent or their authorized representative about the alleged violation related to any provisions of the Act or its associated rules and regulations, and if the respondent -

- If the plea is guilty, the order is passed by the Authority, including the imposition of penalty as per the Act's provisions, the rules and regulations.
- Does not plead guilty and contests the complaint, the Authority shall demand an explanation from the respondent.

In case the Authority is satisfied based on the submissions made in the complaint that the submissions do not require any further inquiry, it may dismiss the complaint.

In case the Authority is satisfied based on the submissions made that there is a need for further hearing, it may order for the documents to be produced or other evidence on a date and time fixed by it.

The Authority shall have the power to carry out an inquiry into the complaint based on the documents and submissions.

The Authority can call upon and compel the presence of any individual familiar with the facts and details of the case to provide testimony or to present any documents that, in the judgment of the Authority, could be beneficial for or related to the subject of the investigation. The Authority is not required to adhere to the regulations of the Indian Evidence Act, 1872 (11 of 1872) while collecting such testimony.

Upon the scheduled date, the Authority will carefully review the evidence presented to it, along with other records and submissions. if satisfied that -

- If the respondent violates the Act or its related rules and regulations, the Authority will make appropriate decisions, including imposing penalties, as per the provisions of the Act or its related rules and regulations, and will provide written reasons for its decision.
- If the respondent is not in violation of the Act or its related rules and regulations, the Authority can reject the complaint in writing, providing recorded reasons for its decision.
- If any individual fails to appear before the Authority, the Authority has the authority to proceed with the inquiry in the unavailability of any such person after documenting the reasons for this action.

Power to Adjudicate by the adjudicating officer

Section 71: Power to Adjudicate

Appointment of Adjudicating Officer:

- The Authority, in consultation with the appropriate Government, appoints one or more judicial officers who are or have been District Judges.
- The appointed officer adjudicates compensation under Sections 12, 14, 18, and 19 of the Act.
- The inquiry process is conducted in the prescribed manner after providing all concerned parties a reasonable opportunity to be heard.

Provision for Pending Complaints:

If a complaint under the Consumer Protection Act, 1986, is pending before a Consumer Disputes Redressal Forum or Commission at the commencement of this Act:

- The complainant may withdraw the complaint with the Forum's or Commission's permission.
- The complainant may then file an application before the adjudicating officer under this Act.

Timeframe for Disposal of Application:

- The adjudicating officer must dispose of applications within 60 days from the receipt date.
- If unable to do so, the officer must record written reasons for the delay.

Investigation and Powers:

- The adjudicating officer has the authority to: Summon individuals with knowledge of case facts or compel testimony or production of documents.
- Upon determining non-compliance with sections specified in subsection (1), the officer can: Direct the payment of suitable compensation or interest, as per the provisions of these sections.

Section 72: Factors Considered in Adjudging Compensation

When determining the quantum of compensation or interest under Section 71, the adjudicating officer evaluates:

1. Unfair Advantage: The amount of any unfair advantage gained by the default, if quantifiable.
2. Loss Caused: The extent of loss caused to the aggrieved party by the default.
3. Repetitive Nature of Default: Whether the default has occurred repeatedly.
4. Other Necessary Factors: Any additional factors required for delivering justice, as deemed necessary by the adjudicating officer.

Manner of holding an inquiry by the Adjudicating officer

Rule 7: Manner of Filing a Complaint with the Adjudicating Officer and Holding an Inquiry

1. Filing a Complaint:

Any aggrieved person may file a complaint with the Adjudicating Officer through the office of the Authority for compensation under Sections **12**, **14**, **18**, and **19** of the Act. The complaint must be submitted in **Form B**, accompanied by a fee of **₹5,000**, payable via **NEFT**, **RTGS**, or any other digital transaction mode.

2. Procedure for Deciding a Complaint:

The Adjudicating Officer shall follow the procedure below for handling complaints:

(a) Issuance of Notice:

Upon receiving a complaint, the Adjudicating Officer issues a notice to the respondent specifying the date and time for a hearing.

(b) Explanation of Allegations:

On the designated date, the Adjudicating Officer explains the alleged violation to the respondent or their authorized representative:

- If the respondent pleads guilty, the officer records the plea and adjudges the quantum of compensation as per the Act's provisions, rules, and regulations.
- If the respondent contests the complaint, the officer demands an explanation.

3. Dismissal of Complaint:

If satisfied based on submissions that no further inquiry is required, the Adjudicating Officer may dismiss the complaint.

4. Order for Further Inquiry:

If the Adjudicating Officer deems further investigation necessary, they may order the production of relevant documents on a specified date and time.

5. Submission of Evidence:

On the fixed date, both the applicant and respondent are required to present relevant evidence and documents beneficial for the inquiry. The officer then inquires into the complaint based on the submissions and documentation.

6. Passing of Orders:

After evaluating the evidence and records, the Adjudicating Officer may:

- Order Compensation: If the respondent is found in violation of the Act or its rules and regulations, the officer passes an order adjudging the quantum of compensation, with reasons recorded in writing.
- Dismiss the Complaint: If no violation is found, the officer dismisses the complaint, with reasons recorded in writing.

7. Proceedings in Absence:

If a person fails, neglects, or refuses to appear as required, the Adjudicating Officer may proceed with the inquiry in their absence, recording the reasons for doing so.

8. Consideration of Factors in Section 72:

Before passing any order, the Adjudicating Officer must consider the factors specified under **Section 72**, including unfair advantage, loss caused, repetitive nature of the default, and other necessary factors for justice.

An adjudicating officer can also provide a remedy for the following:

- Compensation for any degradation of the quality of service or workmanship provided by the promoter. Section 14(3)
- Refund with monthly interest for delayed possession. Section 18(1)
- Refund with interest for any false advertisements/promises made by the promoter.
- Compensation for any changes made in the original plan without the consent of the allottees. Section 14(2)
- Compensation for a defective title. Section 18(2)

- Compensation for any violations of any Acts/rules made by the respondent. Section 18(3)

Process of resolution

1. Assigning the complaint Number and initiating hearings:

Once your complaint is registered under RERA, the Authority will issue a complaint number, which will be used for further reference until your complaint is disposed of. RERA issues a notice to the other parties by email, and the complainant may forward the hearing notice by email or speed post to the respondents immediately upon receipt of the hearing notice. The notice has the complaint number, through which the promoter can preview the complaint filed on the Maha RERA website. The promoter, the allottees, and other concerned parties are then assigned a date within 30-45 days from the date of the complaint registered to initiate the case under RERA.

2. Filing of Documents

Documents needed to certify one's claim include complaint copy, agreement for sale, receipts of the amount paid, tripartite agreement copy if any and other documents relied upon are to be uploaded on the complaint login of Maha RERA.

3. Reply from the Respondent

The respondent is allowed to file his reply to the complaint. The reply should be presented before the Authority or Adjudicating officer through an online complaint login and mentioned during the hearing in the presence of the complainant.

4. Preliminary objections by respondents

Even before filing the reply, the respondents may often challenge the jurisdiction or file preliminary objections, which state that the complaint does not pertain to the project, in hopes of getting the complaint dismissed. The parties file a reply and written submission for such interim applications, if required. The Authority or the Adjudication officer pass orders for such interim applications; they record the order in the roznama, or they pass a detailed interim order and then proceed with the matter.

5. The respondent may file an appeal on interim order

Suppose the respondent wants to frustrate the complainants with multiple litigations. In that case, they may file an appeal u/s 43 before the Maharashtra Real Estate Appellate Tribunal on the Interim order passed by the Authority or the Adjudicating officer. They can buy time by filing such an appeal. If the order of the appellate tribunal is not in their favour, they may proceed to file a second appeal u/s 58, read with Civil Procedure Code 100, before the Hon'ble High Court, and if required, they may find a special leave petition before the Supreme Court also.

6. Final Order

After all arguments are heard from the complainant and the respondent for the final order, the order may take 15-30 days to be released. The order is also posted online on the Maha RERA website.

According to the RERA, once an order is passed, it must be executed within a fixed time. If the respondent fails to honour the order, there are provisions for monetary penalties and imprisonment. Once an order for compensation or refund is issued by RERA and the respondent is unable to follow the said order, an excecution complaint has to be filed against him, within 60 days of the order being passed and the necessary action can then be taken.

Application for rectification of the order

Upon receiving or uploading the order on the Authority's website, the concerned parties have the option to submit a request for the correction of the order.

Correction of order (Section 39 of RERA):

The Authority is empowered to modify any order it has issued within two years from the date of the order under this Act, for the purpose of rectifying any obvious errors in the record.

It is mandatory for the Authority to make such modifications if the errors are brought to its attention by the parties. However, no modifications can be made to an order for which an appeal has been filed under this Act. Furthermore, the Authority is prohibited from altering the substantive part of its order while rectifying any obvious errors in the record under the provisions of this Act.

The Authority or the adjudicating officer has a two-year period to consider the rectification application.

Chapter 2

Appeals under RERA

An appeal is a process by which a subordinate Court's judgment or order is challenged before its superior Court.

The Real Estate Appellate Tribunal (REAT) was set up to make decicions on any appeals made against the orders passed by RERA.

Established under section 43 of RERA, the REAT can examine the legality of RERA orders and decide whether to uphold or overturn them. The decisions or orders of the Appellate Tribunal are subject to appeal in the High Court.

Powers of Appellate Tribunal

Section 53 of RERA states:

(1) The Appellate Tribunal is not required to go according to the Code of Civil Procedure of 1908, but must adhere to the principles of natural justice.

(2) The Appellate Tribunal has the authority to regulate its procedure, subject to the provisions of this Act.

(3) The Appellate Tribunal is not bound by the rules of evidence in the Indian Evidence Act of 1872.

(4) The Appellate Tribunal has the same powers as a civil court as per the Code of Civil Procedure of 1908, when it comes to the functions under this Act, including summoning and examining individuals under oath, demanding the discovery and production of documents, accepting evidence on affidavits, issuing commissions for witness or document examinations, reviewing its decisions, dismissing applications for default or directing them ex parte, and other matters as prescribed.

(5) All proceedings before the Appellate Tribunal are considered judicial proceedings as per sections 193, 219, and 228 of section 196 of the Indian Penal Code. The Appellate Tribunal is treated

as a civil court for section 195 and Chapter XXVI of the Code of Criminal Procedure, 1973.

The Appellate Tribunal has the authority to enlist the assistance of experts or consultants in economics, real estate, accountancy, architecture, law, or any other relevant field to aid in its proceedings.

Right to Appeal

Maha RERA grants the right to appeal when challenging decisions or orders made by Maha RERA. In line with this, the Maharashtra Appellate Tribunal (MREAT) was established to hear appeals against the decisions of Maha RERA.

Section 43(1) of RERA mandates the establishment of an Appellate Tribunal within one year from the commencement date of the RERA authority of the respective state, referred to as the "Real Estate Appellate Tribunal (REAT)" by the State Government. This Appellate Tribunal is a quasi-judicial body empowered to hear appeals from orders, decisions, or directions made by RERA or the Adjudicating Officer.

Maha REAT was established on 8th May 2018 by the Maharashtra Government.

An aggrieved party does not have any inherent right to challenge a judgement or an order made by RERA, as the right to appeal is created by statute. This means that the ability to appeal a decision is granted only when a specific law is passed by a legislative body. Without any law allowing any party to appeal, no one would have the legal standing to appeal a decision.

As reported in a supreme court judgement in 1983, 3 SCC 75, in the case of M/s. M. Ramnarain Private Limited and Anr. V. State Trading Corporation of India Limited, the Hon'ble Supreme Court stated that "the right to prefer an appeal is a right created by statute; no party can file an appeal against any judgment, decree or order as a matter of course in the absence of a suitable provision of some law conferring on the party concerned the right to file an appeal against any judgment, decree or order."

Section 43(5) of RERA states that -

Under RERA, any person aggrieved by a decision of the Authority or the Adjudicating Officer has the right to appeal to the Appellate Tribunal with jurisdiction over the matter. This provision offers a formal avenue for disputing parties to seek a review or modification of the decisions made under the Act, ensuring that there is a mechanism for redressal and accountability.

Conditions for Promoters to File an Appeal:

For a promoter to file an appeal, specific conditions must be met before the appeal is entertained. The promoter is required to deposit to the Appellate Tribunal at least 30% of the penalty imposed, or a higher percentage if determined by the Tribunal. Alternatively, the promoter must deposit the total amount payable to the allottee, including interest and compensation, or both, as applicable. This prerequisite ensures that the promoter demonstrates a genuine commitment to comply with the financial obligations before proceeding with the appeal, thereby preventing frivolous appeals and protecting the interests of allottees.

Purpose of the Deposit Requirement:

The deposit requirement serves as a safeguard to ensure that the promoter takes responsibility for the imposed penalties or compensations while the appeal is pending. It acts as a deterrent against unnecessary appeals and secures a portion of the compensation or penalty for the allottees, thereby providing a balance between the rights of promoters to appeal and the protection of allottees' interests during the dispute resolution process.

Procedure for Filing an Appeal (Section 44 of RERA):

1. Right to Appeal:

- The appropriate Government, the competent Authority, or any person aggrieved by a direction, order, or decision of the RERA Authority or the adjudicating officer can file their appeal before the Appellate Tribunal.

2. Time Frame for Filing an Appeal:

- An appeal has to be filed within 60 days from the date of receiving the copy of the direction, order, or decision from the Authority or adjudicating officer. The appeal should be in the prescribed form and accompanied by the required fee.
- The Appellate Tribunal may accept an appeal even after the 60-day period if it is satisfied that there was a sufficient reason for not filing the appeal within the stipulated time.

3. Hearing and Orders:

Upon receiving an appeal, the Appellate Tribunal can pass orders, including interim orders, as it deems fit after providing both parties the opportunity to be heard.

4. Communication of Orders:

A copy of every order made by the Appellate Tribunal must be sent to the parties involved in the appeal, as well as to the RERA Authority or the adjudicating officer concerned.

5. Expeditious Disposal:

The Appellate Tribunal aims to dispose of the appeal under 60 days from the date of receipt of the appeal. If it cannot do so within this period, it must record the reasons for the delay in writing.

6. Review of Records:

The Appellate Tribunal has the power to call for records to examine the legality, propriety, or correctness of any order or decision made by the RERA Authority or the adjudicating officer. It can do this on its own motion or upon receiving an appeal, and it can make such orders as it deems fit based on its examination.

Rule 9 of Maha RERA states that -

1. Every Appeal filed under section 44(1) shall be accompanied with a sum of five thousand rupees through NEFT or RTGS system or any other digital transaction mode.
2. Every Appeal shall be filed in Form 'C' in triplicate, along with the following documents, -

(a) Attested copy of the concerned order

(b) Copies of the document relevant for the appeal

(c) index of the documents

Provided that, when the Authority makes a provision for filing a complaint web-based, it shall not be necessary to submit such form in triplicate.

Regulation 9 of the Maharashtra Real Estate Appellate Tribunal Regulations, 2019, states that:

1. All appeals instituted with the Tribunal shall be presented online in 'Form C' as prescribed.
2. Every Appeal shall be accompanied by an appeal fee of Rs. 5000/- (Rupees Five Thousand) payable only online.
3. The hard copy of such appeals, along with attachments, shall be presented to the Office of the Registrar to the authorised person within 7 days from the date of online filing. On failure to submit hard copies within time, such appeals shall be notified by the Registry for dismissal for want of hard copies.
4. All other proceedings with attachments, if any, shall be instituted in the Office of the Registrar till the online system is in place.
5. All proceedings to be presented to the Tribunal shall be in English. In case it is in another language, it shall be accompanied by a true translation in English. It shall be legible, type-written or printed in double spacing with proper margin, duly paginated, indexed and stitched together in paper book form, and presented in duplicate.
6. The authorised official, on receipt of proceedings as per (ii), (iii) and (iv) above, shall affix the date and seal of the Tribunal on all pages under his initials and thereafter shall on the same day send to the Registrar.
7. Court fee stamps affixed on Vakalatnama, Letter of Authorisation and the documents shall be checked and entered after due cancellation in the Court Fee Register to be maintained as per the procedure.

8. In case of delay, if the last day of filing an appeal falls on a holiday, that day and succeeding holidays shall be excluded to reckon the limitation period. The appeal should be presented on the next working day, after the holidays, from the last date of the limitation.
9. On examination of appeals, if the Registrar finds the same in order, he shall seek appropriate orders for allotment of appeal.

Regulation 10 of the Maharashtra Real Estate Appellate Tribunal Regulations, 2019, states that –

1. Memorandum of Appeal with attachments with adequate copies to be served on respondents.
2. If an Appeal is presented through an Advocate, the necessary Vakalatnama is duly attested with the necessary court fee stamp and Advocate Welfare Fund Stamp if applicable. Vakalatnama shall contain the address of the advocate, including the enrollment number, email ID, mobile number, etc., for proper communication.
3. If a proceeding is filed by an authorised representative, Chartered Accountant, Cost Accountant or Company Secretary as provided in section 56 of the Act, Power of Attorney or authority letter in original.
4. Certified copy of impugned order.
5. All the documents shall be produced along with the list of documents (Form B).
6. An application for condonation of delay when an Appeal is presented after period of limitation has expired.
7. Other documents, if any, in accordance with the law and rules framed thereunder.

Procedure for filing the second Appeal

Appeals to the High Court

Section 58 of Maha RERA states the following -

Suppose a person is aggrieved by any decision of the Real Estate Appellate Tribunal. In that case, they can file an Appeal within 60 days of the order to the High Court of the respective state or Union Territory, as specified in section 100 of the Code of Civil Procedure, 1908.

1. Right to Second Appeal:

A second appeal can be filed with the High Court against a decree passed in an appeal by any court which is subordinate to the High Court. This is permissible only if the High Court is satisfied that the case involves a substantial question of law. This provision applies unless otherwise explicitly stated in the Code or any other prevailing law.

2. Ex-Parte Decrees:

A second appeal can also be filed against an appellate decree that has been passed ex-parte, allowing for a review of the decision even when the decree was issued without the appellant's presence.

3. Requirement of Substantial Question of Law:

The memorandum of appeal should clearly state the substantial question of law involved in the case. This is a mandatory requirement to ensure that the appeal is based on significant legal issues rather than mere factual disputes.

4. Formulation of Question of Law:

If the High Court is convinced that a substantial question of law exists, it shall explicitly formulate this question. The hearing of the appeal will then focus on the question(s) so formulated.

5. Hearing and Scope of Argument:

During the hearing, the respondent has the right to argue that the case does not involve the substantial question of law formulated by the High Court. However, the High Court retains the authority to hear and decide on any other substantial question of law not initially formulated, provided it records the reasons for doing so and is satisfied that the case indeed involves such a question.

Section (100) Code of Civil Procedure, 1908 allows a second appeal to the High Court from an appellate decree only if the statute provides for a condition that must be satisfied before a court can exercise its appellate jurisdiction.

Section 102 states that if the second Appeal's objective is to recover money, then the amount to be recovered should be greater than the sum of Rs. 25,000. The High Court shall lack the requisite jurisdiction to proceed with the Appeal if it is less than the said amount.

The respondent has the liberty to argue that the Appeal made does not have a question of law and is thus irrelevant.

Documents required to file a second appeal

1. A certified copy of the order or judgement passed by the Appellate Tribunal that is to be challenged.
2. A certified copy of the order or judgement passed by the Maha RERA authority or Adjudicating Officer before the first Appeal.
3. Applicable practice notes (2 sets) are on the High Court Website and verified by the Registry of the High Court.
4. All arguments/complaints and replies recorded prior, as relevant to the second Appeal.
5. Documents filed in the Complaint.
6. Interim Application (if any)
7. Vakalatnama
8. A resolution is needed if a company files the appeal.
9. A Power of Attorney if a second Appeal is filed through a professional.
10. Court fees and Presentation form.

Chapter 3

Execution of Orders

Execution of Orders under RERA:

1. Powers of the Appellate Tribunal (Section 57):

The Appellate Tribunal's orders are enforceable as a decree of a civil court, with all the associated powers of execution. It can either execute the orders itself or transmit them to a civil court with local jurisdiction for execution. This ensures that the orders issued by the Tribunal are treated with the same seriousness and enforceability as those of a civil court.

2. Procedure for Execution (Maha RERA Order No. 15/2020 & Section 63):

The Secretary of Maha RERA holds the power to execute orders. Upon receiving an order, the party in whose favour it is issued must inform the opposing party to comply within the specified timeframe. If the respondent fails to comply with orders involving interest, compensation, or other matters, the judgment creditor can apply on the Maha RERA website to execute the order. Non-compliance by a promoter with Authority orders can result in a daily penalty, up to 5% of the project cost, and imprisonment for repeated violations.

3. Recovery of Monetary Claims (Section 40 & Maha RERA Order No. 44/2023):

If a party fails to pay interest, penalty, or compensation, the recovery can be treated as arrears of land revenue. The concerned Collector's office is responsible for executing recovery warrants issued by MahaRERA. If not executed within six months, the aggrieved party may approach the High Court. The Allahabad High Court has mandated District Magistrates to execute recovery certificates within four weeks. For non-monetary claims, MahaRERA imposes a penalty until the order is complied with. If execution is not possible, the order is sent to the principal civil court within the local jurisdiction for enforcement.

Recovery of Arrears

An arrear of land revenue can be recovered using one or more of the following methods:

1.Notice of Demand (Section 178):

Serving a written notice to the defaulter to inform them of the arrears and require payment.

2. Forfeiture of Occupancy or Alienated Holding (Section 179):

Forfeiting the occupancy or alienated holding (property held in tenure) for which the arrear is due.

3. Distraint and Sale of Movable Property (Section 180):

Seizing and selling the defaulter's movable property.

4. Attachment and Sale of Immovable Property (Section 181):

Attaching and selling the defaulter's immovable property, such as land or buildings.

5. Attachment of Immovable Property (Section 182):

Attaching the defaulter's immovable property without immediate sale.

6. Arrest and Imprisonment (Sections 183 and 184):

Arresting and imprisoning the defaulter as a measure to enforce payment of arrears.

7. Attachment of Entire Villages or Shares of Villages (Sections 185-190):

In cases involving alienated holdings comprising entire villages or shares of villages, the attachment of such villages or shares can be carried out.

Exemptions from Attachment and Sale:

The following items are exempt from attachment and sale under clauses (c), (d), and (e):

1. Essential Items:

Necessary clothing, cooking vessels, beds, bedding for the defaulter, his wife and children, and personal ornaments that cannot be parted with according to religious customs.

2. Tools and Implements:

Tools of artisans and, in the case of agriculturists, their implements of husbandry (excluding those driven by mechanical power) and necessary cattle and seed for earning their livelihood.

3. Religious Articles:

Articles set aside exclusively for religious endowments.

4. Agriculturalist's Residence:

Houses and buildings (along with materials, sites, and land immediately appurtenant) that are owned and occupied by an agriculturist.

Penalties imposed by RERA

The imposition of penalties by Maha RERA aims to guarantee consumer protection, hold developers responsible, and encourage regulatory adherence within the real estate sector. Ethical practices are facilitated by penalties, creating an environment that fosters transparency, market stability, and investor confidence, thereby contributing to a fair and sustainable real estate market.

Offences for which penalties are charged –

1. Failure to declare encumbrance on the land by the Promoter
2. Changes in plans made by the promoter without the consent of the allottees
3. If the promoter tries registering the project under RERA by uploading the IOD instead of a CC.
4. Selling/advertising a project without registration
5. If an advertisement for a project does not include the RERA registration number prominently or provides false information in the advertisements
6. When a promoter fails to carry out the formation of the association of allottees when more than 51% of the flats have been booked
7. Failure of compensation by the promoter to the Allottee

8. Failure to declare ongoing projects when registering a new project
9. If any party does not comply with any orders issued by the Authority

For Allottees:

Allottees must adhere to the orders and directions issued by the RERA Authority and Appellate Tribunal. If the allottees fail to comply, it can lead to penalties being imposed on them. As per Sections 67 and 68, non-compliance can attract a penalty of up to 5% of the cost of the property for violating Authority orders. Continued violations may result in imprisonment of up to one year, a fine of up to 10% of the property's cost, or both, for disobeying Tribunal directives. It is essential for allottees to respect and follow legal decisions to avoid such severe consequences.

For Real Estate Agents:

Real estate agents are required to operate with transparency and comply with the regulations set under RERA, particularly Sections 9 and 10. Violations, such as marketing unregistered projects, can result in daily fines of □10,000, cumulatively up to 5% of the project cost. Additionally, failing to follow orders from the Authority or Appellate Tribunal can lead to further penalties or even imprisonment of up to one year under Sections 65 and 66. Agents must ensure all dealings are within the legal framework to maintain credibility and avoid these penalties.

For Promoters:

Promoters have significant responsibilities under RERA, including mandatory project registration and truthful disclosures. Violating these, especially the registration requirement under Section 3, can lead to a penalty of up to 10% of the project cost and even imprisonment for repeated non-compliance as per Section 59. Further, providing false information or contravening any provisions under the Act may attract penalties up to 5% of the project cost, as stated in Sections 60 and 61. Promoters must conduct business with utmost diligence and transparency to prevent legal and financial repercussions.

Chapter 4

Conciliation and Dispute Resolution

Conciliation involves a process of alternative dispute resolution where conflicting parties seek to resolve their disputes with the assistance of an impartial third party.

According to Section 32 (g) of RERA, the Authority is mandated to recommend measures for facilitating amicable conciliation of disputes between promoters and allottees through dispute settlement forums established by consumer or promoter associations to promote a healthy, transparent, efficient, and competitive real estate sector.

The Conciliator conducts joint and separate meetings with the parties to ensure the attainment of a friendly agreement. This informal process is overseen by a specialized Conciliator in the relevant field. Conciliation is cost-effective and much quicker than litigation, without imposing any binding decisions unless mutually agreed upon and documented. If an agreement cannot be reached, the parties have the option to seek resolution through the Court of law.

The Maha RERA conciliation forum is chaired by the Secretary and includes two representatives each from Mumbai Grahak Panchayat, MCHI, CREDAI, CREDAI—Pune, and NAREDCO, in accordance with order no. 15/2018 of Maha RERA. The Secretary assumes the role of chairperson and holds general supervisory powers over the meetings.

To avail of the conciliation forum, the aggrieved party needs to register on the online portal (https://mahareraconciliation.mahaonline.gov.in) using their login details. Once the necessary procedures are completed on the website and payment is made, a conciliation bench is allocated based on availability. If the conciliation is successful, both parties sign an agreement, effectively resolving the dispute.

Role and Responsibilities of Conciliators

1. To assist the parties individually and impartially to reach an amicable decision.

2. To handle both parties and consider all the points/arguments they put forth.
3. Hold private sessions for the parties, if needed.
4. To come to a solution that is accepted by both the parties.
5. To summarize mutually acceptable decisions

Allottee grievance redressal cell

Order no. 45/2023 of Maha RERA advises the promoters to establish a home buyer/Allottee Redressal Cell. By doing so, allottee disputes can be resolved much faster and can even reduce the stress of many cases on the Authority.

Maha RERA states that every Redressal Cell should have a minimum of 1 Grievance Redressal Officer available to assist the homebuyers. The promoter should also upload the number of complaints filed and resolved on its webpage.

This benefits the promoter, too, as it adds up during the grading system of projects done by Maha RERA.

Part 6

RERA and other Comparative Laws

Chapter 1

Rera vs Consumer Forum vs IBC

A nation's successful economy is supported by its robust real estate market. Not only is the housing industry one of the most attractive sectors for foreign investment, but it also plays a significant role in advancing and developing a country's infrastructure. This industry, like any other, has shortfalls and is vulnerable to difficulties. However, in recent years, this industry has been through turbulence. Many issues, including a lack of transparency, business inefficiencies, and other blunders, have severely harmed this industry.

As a result, the real estate market has suffered, which has seriously impacted the economy and has proven particularly bad for homebuyers. Homebuyers are frequently deceived by failing promoters and subjected to malpractices practised by defaulting promoters, ultimately depleting their life savings invested in the projects. Homebuyers often encounter issues while investing in such developments, despite completing their research and due diligence.

This is where the need for regulating authorities and rules comes into play. An aggrieved buyer currently has three options; the Consumer Protection Act of 1986 (CPA) as a consumer, the Real Estate (Regulation and Development) Act of 2016 (RERA) as an allottee, or the Insolvency and Bankruptcy Code of 2016. (IBC) as a financial creditor.

Homebuyers can pursue legal remedies and relief under the Consumer Protection Act of 1986 (CPA), the Real Estate (Regulation and Development) Act of 2016 (RERA), or the Insolvency and Bankruptcy Code of 2016. (IBC). The remedies offered under the CPA, RERA, and IBC are all concurrent. Although, homebuyers should exercise caution when engaging in various legal procedures; otherwise, instead of resolving a problem swiftly, one may end up greatly prolonging it.

Before RERA was implemented, non-investor homebuyers sought remedies through CPA consumer forums. This was an effective cure at an era when most builders were not over-leveraged, and the financial sector was not affected by the turpitude of the real estate market. RERA was introduced largely to give a dedicated platform for allottees to air their issues and save the project a developer is constructing.

Real Estate (Regulation and Development) Act (RERA)

"The Real Estate (Regulation and Development) Act aims to create national standards across the country to safeguard home buyers' interests, as well as to promote transparency in construction company operations and lower the likelihood of default or misappropriation of funds by builders."

RERA is the first regulator to control the Indian real estate market. It aims to bring clarity and fair business practices that protect buyers' interests and streamline the Real Estate operating framework, resulting in buyers' interest in completed and ready-to-move-in properties.

Before the implementation of RERA, India's real estate sector faced numerous challenges, such as obtaining approvals, a lack of clear land ownership, speculation in property prices, and the list went on and on.

Additionally, customers had little protection against issues such as project delays, limited or no compensation from the government, and unjustifiable interest charges. According to the Act, real estate developers cannot market or sell any apartments or units without registering the project with the appropriate RERA authorities. It requires developers to complete construction and handover of units on time, failing which buyers can exit the project and demand a refund of monies with interest. Any aggrieved party may file a complaint with the RERA Authority for a promoter violating the act's provisions.

This act authorises and protects the buyer's right to enquire about all aspects of a real estate project and to review project documentation. It serves as a customer data bank, regulator, and observer, ensuring project transparency and completion on schedule. By its structure, RERA has a broad scope. It encompasses both commercial and residential projects, providing homebuyers with comprehensive protection. This statute applies to all parties involved in a real estate transaction, including brokers and agents. RERA requires builders to enter the project completion deadline at the time of registration.

Unnecessary delays and failure to meet the deadline would result in penalties as well as criminal proceedings. A key disadvantage that existed before the introduction of this act and was a major source of project delays and non-completion was that builders used to move cash from an ongoing project to a new project. RERA has addressed this by requiring builders to deposit 70% of the funds in a separate bank account to be used in the project for which they were sanctioned and not diverted to a new project. The act establishes an Appellant System for Grievance Redressal and penalties and sanctions for defaulters.

Consumer Protection Act of 1986 (CPA)

"The Consumer Protection Act of 1986 (CPA) was implemented to provide a prompt redressal mechanism to consumers who claimed Unfair Trade Practices or Inadequacies with respect to Goods or Services - home buyers were also included within the purview of the Act by interpreting the term "Services" under the Act to include construction."

The National Consumer Disputes Redressal Commission (NCDRC) of India is a quasi-judicial commission established in 1988 by the Consumer Protection Act of 1986. When filing a consumer complaint, you must do so within the time limits specified. District commissions can hear complaints worth Rs 1 crore, whereas state commissions can hear complaints worth Rs 10 crore. One must approach the NCDRC if the property is worth over INR 10 crore.

The Consumer Protection Act of 1986 is renowned social legislation establishing consumer rights and offering protection and promotion. It was the first act of this kind in India, allowing ordinary consumers to obtain less expensive and often faster redressal of their complaints. At each District, State, and National level, quasi-judicial bodies known as District Commissions, State Consumer Disputes Redressal Commissions, and National Consumer Redressal Commissions have been established. The National Commission has the authority to issue directives on the following:

1. Adoption of a standardised procedure for hearing the cases,
2. Providing copies of documents created by one party before serving them to the opposing parties,
3. Prompt provision of document copies

4. They generally supervise the State Commissions and District Commissions to ensure that the act's objects and purposes are best served without infringing on their quasi-judicial freedom.

In addition to RERA, buyers can also approach the consumer forum for compensation for their grievances. According to the Supreme Court, home buyers can go to the consumer forum to seek redress from builders, such as refunds and compensation for delays in handing over possession. A home buyer can also sue the builder in consumer court for false advertising, a felony under consumer protection law.

If convicted, the developer could face up to two years in prison and a monetary penalty of up to Rs 10 lakhs. The penalty may be increased to Rs 50 lakhs and imprisonment for up to five years. Despite being promised protection under the sector-specific RERA, home buyers continue to approach consumer commissions due to the high rate of justice delivery.

Insolvency and Bankruptcy Board of India (IBC)

"The Insolvency and Bankruptcy Code, one of the best methods for timely money recovery and the revival of failing businesses, also covered project's allottees and declared them to be financial creditors for purposes of the Act, giving aggrieved Indian homebuyers an alternative option."

On October 1, 2016, the Insolvency and Bankruptcy Board of India was formed under the Insolvency and Bankruptcy Codes. It is crucial in enforcing the Code, consolidating and amending corporate restructuring laws and resolving insolvency for individuals, partnership firms, and corporations. To further the goals of the Code, IBC has recently given the mandate to encourage the growth of and regulate the working practices of insolvent professionals, agencies, and information utilities.

Insolvency and Bankruptcy Board of India have requested advice on critical matters of public interest in real estate firm bankruptcy. These inputs include how to treat buyers who have not yet moved into their new residences if corporate rescue efforts fail and the real estate firm eventually becomes liquidated. It is an essential issue because it pertains to the rights of various home buyers based on their purchase status.

IBBI is looking for inputs on whether it is necessary to re-evaluate the position of the authorised representative of home buyers in the panel of creditors determining the future of the bankrupt company. Whether specific real estate projects of an insolvent developer require separate authorised agents from home, buyers must also be considered. It effectively gives homebuyers the choice of filing for admission into the Corporate Insolvency Resolution Process (CIRP) under IBC or seeking relief under RERA.

Whom to approach?

RERA v CPA

Before 2017, no central regulator in India and state regulations applied to the sale of units in projects still under development. The Central Government subsequently published the Real Estate (Regulation & Development) Act 2016, giving homebuyers a dedicated platform for pursuing legal recourse. The Consumer Protection Act's consumer forums are explicitly included in the act's scope of authority. The Supreme Court has provided an answer to this query in the "Imperia Structures vs Anil Patni and another" case.

The Consumer Protection Act prohibits civil courts from having jurisdiction over cases that may bring before the RERA Authority. If a developer fails to provide adequate services, allottees of any project—regardless of whether it is registered as a "real-estate project" under RERA—have the right to file a complaint with the National Consumer Dispute Redressal Forum (NCDRC).

The act was created to protect consumers' interests and ensure that the sale of a plot, apartment, or unit in an Indian real estate project is conducted effectively and transparently. Any harmed party may report a promoter's breach or infringement of the act's provisions to the RERA Authority. Homebuyers are free to choose the appropriate forum to present their claims. They must first assess their claims' nature, complexity, and level of final relief. But the consumer forum has its limitations.

1. The NCDRC cannot take action until a consumer complains. It is also not allowed to conduct an investigation. The Real Estate Regulatory Authority is an exception to this rule (RERA).

2. The NCDRC considers complaints with a value greater than Rs 1 crore. If a buyer must complain against a developer and the total sum at issue is less than Rs 1 crore, they must first seek justice at the district and state levels before approaching the NCDRC. But in a significant decision last year, the Supreme Court stated that buyers could band together and establish groups to petition the apex court directly.
3. In contrast to the RERA, only a registered agency or consumer may file a complaint with the NCDRC.
4. The NCDRC cannot sentence a defaulting developer to prison; it may simply fine him. The RERA, on the other hand, has the power to punish or imprison a promoter who is in default. It may also decide to carry out both.

RERA v IBC

The Insolvency and Bankruptcy Code (IBC) was formed to effect a cultural shift in India's insolvency and bankruptcy landscape. Lenders were happy and grateful for the RERA's passage because it established checks and balances from their point of view, ensuring the completion of real estate projects, facilitating sales, and ultimately enabling the repayment of loans to lenders. Allottees and homebuyers continue to gain the most from the RERA.

Homebuyers can now participate in resolution procedures against real estate developers thanks to new provisions added to the IBC that specifically include them as creditors. Unfortunately, including homeowners as financial creditors in the IBC has exacerbated the law's complex tensions and misunderstandings.

The RERA Act, 2016 and the IBC are fundamentally in conflict since one aims to prioritise creditors while the other seeks to put consumers before creditors. RERA was to enact "control and formalise the real estate sector," but IBC was approved to make "closing the business" easier. The Court determined that RERA must yield to the IBC in the case of a disagreement and that the IBC and RERA must coexist even via a process of harmonious construction.

In conclusion, IBC might not be the best vehicle to address the various complaints of homebuyers, and organisations like RERA would be more appropriate. The legislation may need to balance buyers' interests under RERA and creditors under IBC. Although it remains the second-largest industry for IBC petition filings, real estate is still where these petitions are filed most frequently.

RERA v CPA v IBC

Lawmakers have considered homeowners' concerns and developed several laws that adjudicate their issues and preserve the consumer's interests as the keystone in various court rulings. Adjudicators are also willing to go the extra mile to secure justice. If any statute and the IBC clash, Section 238 of the IBC takes precedence. Section 89 of RERA further specifies that if any law contradicts with RERA, RERA takes precedence. It indicates no "inconsistencies" between RERA and IBC that they work in distinct contexts and serve different purposes.

	RERA	**CPA**	**IBC**
When can the case be filed?	If units are not delivered by the due date	Upon the builder's failure to deliver over possession of the unit or any other service deficiency	In the event of a project delivery failure
Who can file?	A purchaser, home buyer, or potential purchaser/home buyer offered a flat may register a complaint, regardless of whether the person is a corporate entity or an individual.	A Consumer who meets the requirements of Section 2(d) of the CPA may file a CPA complaint. When an individual agrees to purchase a flat for personal use and habitation, he has the right to complain.	Any person, whether an individual or corporate entity, may submit an insolvency application under Section 7 of the IBC. The project allottee is regarded as a financial creditor.

	RERA	CPA	IBC
Appellate Structure	• Real Estate Regulatory Authority; • Real Estate Appellate Tribunal; • High Court; • Supreme Court.	• District Forum; • State Forum; • National Forum; • Supreme Court.	• National Company Law Tribunal; • National Company Law Appellate Tribunal; • Supreme Court.
Requirements to file	Any homebuyer may make a complaint if one of the following three things is not met: (1) handing over possession; (2) a quality concern; or (3) any other violation of RERA's rules.	Any homebuyer (being a customer) may bring a claim if the builder is in default regarding (1) possession, (2) a quality issue, or (3) any other deficiency of service.	If there is a failure to transfer possession, the NCLT must receive a joint application from 10 percent of allottees, or 100 allottees, whichever is fewer.
Case Timeline	Depending on the State, the RERA grievance resolution process can take several months to several years.	A dispute resolution or adjudication by a consumer forum often takes 5 to 6 years.	IBC requires an adjudicating authority to rule on an insolvency application for six months to 1 year.
Overrides	No overriding	No overriding	All laws, including RERA and CPA, are subordinate to the IBC.

	RERA	CPA	IBC
Accessibility	Each state that has established the authority under the act has 1–2 RERA offices.	Every district in the state has a district forum created. Each state's capital serves as the State Commission's seat, while it occasionally has seats in other areas. The National Commission has circuit benches that rotate throughout the country and is presided over in Delhi.	In India, NCLT has 16 benches. The NCLT is often established for each state and sits in one location, or one NCLT is frequently given authority and has jurisdiction over two states.
Nature of Order	If a default is established, a court order is issued requiring the builder to hand over the property or issue a refund.	If a default is established, a court order is issued requiring the builder to hand over the property or issue a refund.	If a default is established, an IRP is appointed for the business, and IRP is given control over all assets and liabilities.
Builders' potential for appeal	After submitting 30% of the amount, an appeal can be filed with the RERA Tribunal.	An appeal may be lodged with the higher consumer court.	Builder company promoters may file an appeal with the NCLT, but the company will be managed by the court-appointed IRP.

	RERA	CPA	IBC
Reliefs provided	RERA normally exercises its authority by issuing an order to levy a fine, deregister the project, including the promoter on a list of defaulters, direct completion of the project in the manner specified in conjunction with the State Government, and issue incidental orders.	The Consumer Forum has the authority to carry out its orders. This expedites the execution of orders compared to conventional cases or the implementation of orders passed by multiple Courts/Quasi-Judicial Forums. Furthermore, because the scope of the Consumer Act is limited, relief and, as a result, implementation is comparably quick.	Once the NCLT accepts the Insolvency Application, the IRP oversees the company's affairs. If the Corporate Insolvency Resolution Process ("CIRP") fails (in the case of the developer being a Corporate Entity), liquidation is initiated. NCLT supervises the entire process, and numerous reports must be filed with NCLT regularly.
Success Rate	20%	10%	99%

	RERA	CPA	IBC
Challenges to Homebuyers	(1) Receiving an order for a refund (2) carrying out the order (3) certain projects not even being registered under RERA (4) and generally, the builder disobeying the directives.	(1) Difficult to demonstrate that the authorised unit will be utilised for commercial purposes; (2) Obtaining a refund order (3) Execution of an order (3) Generally, the builder disobeys orders	(1) Min. 10% of total allottees required (2) Appointment of a good Advocate (3) Finding an efficient IRP
Risks for the builders	Execution of order	Execution of order	(1) The builder will lose control of the project and all of its assets. A new builder will be held accountable for the timely completion of the project; (2) the builder will be unable to reclaim ownership of his company; and (3) the builder will be subjected to forensic audit and other scrutiny in order to uncover fraudulent conduct/ transactions by the builder.

1. Suppose a person is a consumer seeking execution of statutory obligations or compensation. In that case, the Consumer Forum is a better and more effective remedy, especially if the developer can pay. He may also submit a complaint with RERA to blacklist the developer and obtain other reliefs that RERA may supply but the consumer forum cannot.
2. RERA will be a better treatment if a person is not a consumer.
3. If a person is not a consumer and wants the developer to meet statutory requirements, his only option is to bring an ordinary suit. He may, however, seek RERA for compensation and other reliefs.
4. When a developer's financial situation is deteriorating and a person—consumer or not—is only interested in getting his money back, filing an insolvency petition with the NCLT is the best course of action. This is especially true when the property is developed without selling many apartments.
5. RERA would also be a more effective remedy the nearer the project is to completion, particularly if a home buyer wants to buy a flat and vice versa, considering that RERA can also offer compensatory reliefs.
6. When a flat buyer believes the developer's financial situation is worsening and the developer won't be able to finish the project and repay the money with interest to stop future deterioration, insolvency can always be used as an alternative solution. It will make it easier to get back the most money you invested plus interest. Due to many practical challenges that may develop during project completion, completion may take several years. Additionally, if the developer lacks the financial means to pay the order, it will be useless to carry it out.
7. Suppose there is a strong likelihood that the developer won't be able to repay the money invested. In that case, insolvency will be a more profitable remedy in terms of execution because it is a procedure to liquidate the assets of a business or person. Due to their ability to enforce their instructions, consumer forums can offer excellent recourse when a builder has finished their work

but has delayed giving customers their possession or disregarded a legal requirement to do both.

8. Anytime a developer commits fraud, or other criminal offences or activities, a flat or home buyer can file a criminal complaint against them.

It is clear from the analysis above that:

- IBC provides the greatest solution for displeased homebuyers of projects that the builder has delayed or abandoned. IBC revitalises the entire project/company through NCLT.
- RERA is appropriate for projects when there is a minimal amount of construction delay or when there are any other inconsistencies about demand notices and payment schedules.
- Only initiatives that would be outside the purview of RERA are appropriate for the consumer court.

The Real Estate Regulatory Authority (RERA) allows homebuyers to receive compensation for losses or damages they have incurred due to misleading or inaccurate statements or information in project prospectuses. The homebuyer will receive a full refund of his investment plus interest calculated at the statutory rate.

Consumer Protection Act (CPA) states that the purchaser of a home may be entitled to a refund, If the Forum determines that the allegations in the complaint against the services are true, it will issue an order to the opposing party directing him to pay back the fees paid by the complainant along with interest.

Under the **Insolvency and Bankruptcy Board of India (IBC)**, homeowners may apply if a developer (a corporate debtor) has defaulted (100 or 10 per cent of the total number of allottees in the same project). The Corporate Insolvency Resolution Process (CIRP) starts after such an application is accepted.

Only RERA, nor Consumer Redressal Forum or IBC, can offer the following relief:

- RERA may give instructions for project completion after consulting with the relevant State Governments.
- The blacklisting of defaulting builders and developers by RERA prevents them from starting new projects.
- RERA is open to everyone, including non-consumers.

Chapter 2

Rera and Allied Laws

Along with RERA, different laws for real estate are administered in India at the Central, State and local level. These laws affect all the real estate transactions and businesses that take place within the country. They protect the owner's property rights to purchase and sell real estate. The issues covered under these laws are:

- Legal agreements and contracts;
- Creating a plan and keeping track of a real estate project;
- Real estate property possession, distribution, or conflict resolution;
- Drafting deeds and contracts for real estate transactions;
- Support for legal issues related to real estate foreclosure sales;
- Purchasing, selling, acquiring, leasing, and disposing of various kinds of real estate assets;
- Difficulties regarding real estate taxes.

The laws governed by the Central Government are:

1. The Indian Contract Act, 1872
2. The Indian Evidence Act, 1872
3. The Transfer of Property Act, 1882
4. The Indian Easements Act, 1882
5. Power of Attorney Act, 1882
6. The Land Acquisition Act, 1894
7. The Indian Stamp Act, 1899
8. The Co-operative Societies Act, 1912
9. The Wealth Tax Act, 1957
10. Income-tax Act, 1961
11. The Specific Relief Act, 1963

12. The Urban Land (Ceiling and Regulation) Act, 1976
13. The Arbitration and Conciliation Act, 1996
14. Foreign Exchange Management Act, 1999 / Foreign Direct Investment Policy
15. The Multi-State Co-operative Societies Act, 2002
16. Securitization and Reconstruction of Financial Assets and Enforcement of Security Interest Act, 2002
17. Securitization and Reconstruction of Financial Assets and Enforcement of Security Interest Rules, 2011
18. Right to Fair Compensation and Transparency in Land Acquisition, Rehabilitation and Resettlement Act, 2013
19. Real Estate (Regulations and Development) Act, 2016
20. Insolvency and Bankruptcy Code, 2016
21. Goods and Services Tax Act, 2017
22. The Consumer Protection Act, 1986 and 2019
23. SEBI norms for Real Estate Mutual Funds

Some of the salient Acts are:

Maharashtra Ownership Flats Act, 1963 (MOFA)

During 1961, Maharashtra witnessed several malpractices in the real estate sector, such as the bogus sale of flats, low-quality construction, delays in completing projects and mistrust within the industry. This led to the formulation of the Maharashtra Apartment Ownership Act, one of the first forms of regulatory bodies attempted by the government to manage property ownership in Maharashtra. This was when the terms Flat, Carpet Area and Promoter were first defined. The Act laid down the responsibilities of the real estate developers/builders/promoters and the rights of the flat purchasers within the state.

MOFA and RERA

- MOFA was enacted and implemented by the State Government to regulate flats' construction, promotion, sales and management only. In contrast, the Central Government enacted and implemented RERA to cover the whole real estate sector including flats, plots, etc.

- The registration of the projects was not mandatory in MOFA, whereas it is compulsory to register with RERA.
- The carpet area in MOFA had balconies, and only a net usable area was included. In contrast, in RERA, the internal walls are included, and the areas covered by the external walls, exclusive balconies, verandahs, service shafts and terraces are excluded.
- The defect liability period increased from 3 years in MOFA to 5 years in RERA.
- The maximum advance to be given before the execution of the agreement was 20% of the purchase price in MOFA which was reduced to 10% in RERA.
- In the Agreement of sale, the defects covered were mainly structural in MOFA, but RERA also added defects in quality, workmanship and provision of services in this clause.
- Modifications in plans required 100% consent in MOFA which changed to 66.66% in RERA.
- There were no provisions for unfinished projects in MOFA, which changed to takeover of the project by another developer in RERA.

Maharashtra Apartment Ownership Act, 1970

The Maharashtra Apartment Ownership Act aims to create ownership of a single apartment and make it an inheritable and transferable property. The Maharashtra Ownership of Flats Act remains an important legislation intended to build real estate developer behaviour where the project is carried out through the transfer of rights and responsibilities; the latter focuses on determining the ownership of each apartment in the building. MOFA also regulates the sale, transfer and management of under-construction properties, whereas MAOA manages the common areas in the complex as per the by-laws given in the Act.

Development Control and Promotion Regulations

The development control regulations in India are made by the Regional Town Planning authorities of all the State Governments to regulate the development in the states. These development rules set down base standards to be followed by the developers for all civil projects. For the sanction of any project by RERA, it is mandatory to submit the details of the promoters, land details, layout plans, approvals, etc. The development plans help set down guidelines for the verification of these details. Hence, DCPR plays a very important role in RERA.

Some important regulations to refer to in the DCPR of any state are:

- Development charges
- Floor Space Index (FSI) or Floor Area Ratio (FAR) which helps determine the total built up area based on the plot area.
- Transfer of Development (TDR) rights that allows the transfer of balance FSI.
- Road Setbacks and Open Space requirements
- Road widening proposals as per proposed development plan of the area. The existing land use map and the proposed development maps are made every 20 years that define the changes in the city.
- The minimum requirements for designing habitable spaces.

Prevention of Money Laundering Act, 2002

The Money Laundering Prevention Act 2002 is an Indian parliamentary law enacted to prevent money laundering and regulate the confiscation of money laundering assets. PMLA and the rules notified therein came into effect on 1 July 2005. The laws and regulations notified therein require banking companies, financial institutions, and intermediaries to verify the identity of their customers, keep records, and provide information in a prescribed format. India and has three main purposes:

- Prevention and management of money laundering
- Seize and confiscate property obtained from money laundered money

- Addressing all other issues related to money laundering in India

Under Section 2 of the PMLA Act, "reporting entity" means a banking company, financial institution, intermediary, or person engaged in a particular business or profession. Section 12 of the PMLA Act requires the reporting entity to maintain a record of the business under the provisions of the PMLA Act and PMLA Rules 2005.

The real estate broker/agent has to adhere to the Know Your Client ("KYC") standard, conduct proper KYC verification of the client under PMLA Rules 2005 and have the appropriate mechanism to detect and maintain records of suspicious transactions. In addition, the real estate broker/agent must report transactions that meet the criteria for the PMLA Rules 2005 outlined in the Regulation to the PMLA authorities within the specified time period.

The Benami Transaction (Prohibition) Act, 1988

These Benami transactions are properties under the name of another person or a fictitious person. The Benami Transaction (Prohibition) Act & the Prohibition of Benami Property Transaction Rules, 2016, came into force on 1-11-2016. This law was formulated and executed to confiscate all Benami properties and punish the offenders.

Benami transaction is defined under Sec. 2(9) of the Benami Transaction (Prohibition) Act, 1988 as

- Transaction or an arrangement—

a) Where a property is transferred to, or is held by, a person, and the consideration for such property has been provided, or paid by, another person; and

b) The property is held for the immediate or future benefit, direct or indirect, of the person who has provided the consideration, except when the property is held by—

i. a Karta, or a member of a Hindu undivided family, as the case may be, and the property is held for his benefit or benefit of other members in the family, and the consideration for such property has been provided or paid out of the known sources of the Hindu undivided family;

ii. a person standing in a fiduciary capacity for the benefit of another person towards whom he stands in such capacity and includes a trustee, executor, partner, director of a company, a depository or a participant as an agent of a depository under the Depositories Act, 1996 and any other person as may be notified by the Central Government for this purpose;

iii. any person being an individual in the name of his spouse or the name of any child of such individual, and the consideration for such property has been provided or paid out of the known sources of the individual:

iv. any person in the name of his brother or sister or lineal ascendant or descendant, where the names of brother or sister or lineal ascendant or descendant and the individual appear as joint-owners in any document; and the consideration for such property has been provided or paid out of the known sources of the individual: or

- A transaction or an arrangement in respect of a property carried out or made in a fictitious name; or
- A transaction or an arrangement in respect of a property where the owner of the property is not aware of or denies knowledge of such ownership;
- A transaction or an arrangement in respect of a property where the person providing the consideration is not traceable or is fictitious.

The Act punishes offenders with up to seven years of jail and a fine of 25% of the FMV. Factors that are crucial in determining Benami transactions are:

- The source from which the purchase money came;
- The nature of arid possession of the property after the purchase;
- Motive, if any, for giving the transaction a benami colour;
- The position of the parties and the relationship, if any, between the claimant and the alleged benamidar;
- The custody of the title deeds after the sale; and.

- The conduct of the parties concerned in dealing with the property after the sale.

The Foreign Exchange Management Act, 1999

The Foreign Exchange Management Act of 1999 was enacted to integrate and change foreign exchange law to facilitate foreign trade and payments and promote order, development and maintenance of India's foreign exchange market. This is the central law dealing with foreign investments in India.

Section 6 of FEMA covers capital account transactions. Purchase of real estate in India or outside India is generally a capital account transaction. Sec. 6(3) says without prejudice to the generality of the provisions of sub-section (2), the Reserve Bank may, by regulations, prohibit, restrict or regulate the following:

- Transfer of immovable property outside India, other than a lease not exceeding 5 years, by a person resident in India;
- Acquisition or transfer of immovable property in India, other than a lease not exceeding 5 years, by a person resident outside India;

Section 6 (4) of FEMA says that a person (as defined in FEMA) residing in India may own, hold, transfer or invest foreign currency, foreign securities or real estate outside India if the person/individual acquires or inherits such property by someone residing in India. In addition, Section 6 (5) confirms the reversal of Section 6 (4), where non-residents of India can hold, own, transfer or invest in foreign currency, foreign securities or real estate located in India acquired, owned or inherited while living in India. Only under these circumstances can someone who is a non-resident or resident can own real estate in India. Those who violate these reserves may be subject to a contractual penalty of up to three times the amount in question. Such infringement and the value of responding to such infringement is forfeiting their property in India.

Citizens of Pakistan, Bangladesh, Sri Lanka, Afghanistan, China, Iran, Nepal, Bhutan, Macau and Hong Kong, regardless of their residence status, are allowed to acquire real estate in India only with the prior consent of RBI.

Some guidelines for purchasing properties by Non-Resident Indian (NRI)/Person of Indian Origin (PIO) are:

- NRI and PIO are free to acquire real estate via gift either by a PIO, NRI or a resident of India.
- Indian Agricultural Land / Plantation Properties / Farms cannot be purchased or gifted.
- Foreigners of the non-Indian origin or who do not live in India are not allowed to obtain Indian real estate by purchase or gift. However, there are no restrictions on purchasing real estate overseas by residents of India with a lease term of 5 years or less.
- NRI / PIO / Foreigners from other than India can inherit real estate in India.
- A PIO may sell / gift real estate in India (excluding farmland/plantation/farmhouse) to Indian Residents or NRI or PIO with prior approval of RBI.
- NRI / PIO are allowed to sell/donate farmland/plantation assets/farms in India only to residents of India who are citizens of India.

Part 7

Taxes and Additional laws

Chapter 1

Central Advisory Council

Section 41 – Establishment of the Central Advisory Council

1. **Establishment of the Central Advisory Council:** The Central Government, through a notification, may establish a body known as the Central Advisory Council, effective from a date specified in the notification.
2. **Chairperson of the Council:** The Union Minister in charge of the Ministry handling Housing and Urban Affairs shall serve as the ex officio Chairperson of the Central Advisory Council.
3. **Composition of the Council:** The Council will comprise representatives from various ministries and organizations, including:
   - Ministry of Finance
   - Ministry of Industry and Commerce
   - Ministry of Urban Development
   - Ministry of Consumer Affairs
   - Ministry of Corporate Affairs
   - Ministry of Law and Justice
   - Niti Aayog
   - National Housing Bank
   - Housing and Urban Development Corporation
4. **Additionally, the Council will include:**
   - Five representatives from State Governments, chosen by rotation.
   - Five representatives from Real Estate Regulatory Authorities, selected by rotation.
   - Representatives from any other Central Government department as notified.
5. **Representation from the Real Estate Sector:** The Council shall also include up to ten members representing the interests of various stakeholders such as:

- The real estate industry
- Consumers
- Real estate agents
- Construction labourers
- Non-governmental organizations (NGOs)
- Academic and research bodies involved in the real estate sector

Section 42 – Functions of the Central Advisory Council

1. **Advisory Role of the Council:** The Central Advisory Council is tasked with advising and giving recommendations to the Central Government on the following matters:
2. **Implementation of the Act:** Guiding on all issues related to the effective implementation of the Real Estate (Regulation and Development) Act.
3. **Policy Matters:** Offering insights and recommendations on major policy questions affecting the real estate sector.
4. **Consumer Protection:** Suggesting measures to safeguard consumer interests within the real estate industry.
5. **Sectoral Growth and Development:** Promoting strategies and initiatives for fostering the growth and development of the real estate sector.
6. **Additional Matters:** Addressing any other issues or tasks assigned to the Council by the Central Government.
7. **Implementation of Recommendations:** The Central Government may formulate rules and regulations to implement the recommendations made by the Central Advisory Council on the matters mentioned in sub-section (1).

These sections establish the Central Advisory Council as a key body for providing expert advice and recommendations to the Central Government on various aspects of the real estate sector, ensuring a well-regulated and consumer-friendly environment.

Chapter 2

Taxation under RERA

1. Goods and Services Tax (GST)

GST remains a key tax in real estate transactions, with its applicability varying based on the construction stage and property type:

- Under-Construction Properties: 1% for affordable housing (priced under ₹45 lakh, with up to 60 sq.m. carpet area in metros or 90 sq.m. in non-metros) and 5% for non-affordable housing (without input tax credit).

GST is levied on the property's total value, excluding the cost of land, with a one-third deduction for land.

- Ready-to-Move-In Properties: For properties that have received a completion certificate, GST does not apply. These properties are taxed only under stamp duty and registration laws.

2. Income Tax Benefits for Homebuyers

Homebuyers can still avail of several income tax benefits under the Income Tax Act, 1961:

- Section 80C: Deductions of upto ₹1.5 lakh on principal repayment of a home loan.
- Section 24(b): Deductions of up to ₹2 lakh on interest payments for self-occupied properties.
- Section 80EEA: For first-time buyers, an additional deduction of upto ₹1.5 lakh on interest payments for properties priced up to ₹45 lakh.

These benefits help reduce the total cost of homeownership for buyers financing their purchase with loans.

3. Stamp Duty and Registration

Stamp duty is a tax levied on property transactions and is a significant cost for homebuyers. In Maharashtra, the stamp duty rates vary based on the location of the property:

- Mumbai, Pune, and other Urban Areas: The stamp duty rate is 6% of the property's agreement value.
- Breakdown: This includes 5% stamp duty and a 1% metro cess, introduced for metro infrastructure development.
- Rural Areas: In less urbanized areas, the stamp duty rate is 4% of the property's value.

Concessions for Women Buyers

Maharashtra offers a 1% concession on stamp duty for properties registered in the name of female buyers. For example, a woman purchasing a property in Mumbai would pay 5% stamp duty instead of 6%. This concession is aimed at encouraging women's ownership in real estate.

Registration Fees in Maharashtra

In Maharashtra, the registration fee is a standard 1% of the property value or ₹30,000, whichever is lower. This fee is charged for officially registering the sale deed with the government, making the property transaction legally binding.

- For most properties, especially in urban areas like Mumbai and Pune, the registration fee will typically cap at ₹30,000 due to the high property values in these locations.
- For lower-valued properties, the 1% rule will apply if the property's value is below ₹30 lakh.

Online Payment and E-Registration in Maharashtra

Maharashtra offers e-payment facilities for stamp duty and registration charges, simplifying the process for buyers. The Maharashtra Department of Registration and Stamps provides an online portal where homebuyers can pay these fees before physically registering the property.

Chapter 3

RERA in Unison with Legacy Laws

While we have already covered some above, this provides a comprehensive analysis of the laws and RERA unison

1. Maharashtra Ownership Flats Act (MOFA), 1963

MOFA was one of the first laws designed to regulate the promotion, construction, and sale of flats in Maharashtra. It aimed to protect homebuyers by ensuring that developers disclose clear terms regarding the sale, possession, and other details of the property.

Key Provisions:

- Developers must execute a registered agreement before accepting more than 20% of the sale price.
- Obligates the developer to form a society or cooperative housing association for apartment owners.
- Developers must disclose full project details, including sanctioned plans, and any changes must be approved by buyers.

MOFA was often criticized for not being stringent enough in enforcement, leading to the eventual implementation of RERA.

2. Maharashtra Apartment Ownership Act (MAOA), 1970

MAOA governs apartment ownership in Maharashtra, allowing each apartment in a building to be treated as a separate entity, with individual titles granted to flat owners. Unlike MOFA, which emphasizes forming housing societies, MAOA encourages apartment owners' associations.

Key Provisions:

- Facilitates the registration of an apartment deed in the name of the owner.
- Protects buyers by defining apartment ownership rights in relation to common areas, such as land, staircases, and parking.

3. Consumer Protection Act (CPA)

It is designed to protect consumers from unfair trade practices, deficiency of services, or misleading advertisements across all sectors, including real estate. Homebuyers could approach consumer forums under the CPA to seek compensation for issues like delays in possession, defects in construction, or false representations by the builder.

Key Provisions:

- Defines unfair practices in real estate.
- Buyers can file complaints in Consumer Dispute Redressal Commissions for compensation.
- CPA can still be used for compensation claims alongside RERA, but for disputes regarding project completion, transparency, or agreement terms, RERA is now the primary recourse for buyers.

4. Insolvency and Bankruptcy Code (IBC), 2016

IBC was introduced to resolve insolvency issues in a time-bound manner and includes specific provisions for real estate. Under IBC, homebuyers are now recognized as financial creditors, which means they have a say in insolvency proceedings when a developer becomes insolvent.

Key Provisions:

- Homebuyers are considered creditors in insolvency proceedings and can initiate insolvency processes against the developer.
- Gives homebuyers the right to claim refunds or participate in the insolvency resolution process.
- While RERA regulates ongoing projects and ensures project completion, IBC deals with the insolvency of developers. In case of insolvency, IBC takes precedence because it governs the resolution of financial distress.
- Homebuyers can file claims under both RERA and IBC, but IBC will prevail for insolvency-related matters.

5. Prevention of Money Laundering Act (PMLA), 2002

PMLA regulates the use of illicit funds in real estate transactions and aims to prevent money laundering. Under this law, developers and buyers are required to disclose the source of funds used in real estate purchases.

Key Provisions:

- Scrutinizes large transactions to ensure they are not proceeds of crime.
- Requires developers to follow Know Your Customer (KYC) norms for homebuyers.
- RERA requires developers to provide full disclosure of their funding sources and project costs, which complements PMLA's goal of transparency in real estate transactions. If money laundering is suspected, PMLA will prevail in terms of criminal investigation and seizure of assets.

6. Benami Transactions (Prohibition) Act, 1988

The Benami Act prohibits transactions where property is held by one person, but the payment is made by another, which can be used for concealing illegal wealth.

Key Provisions:

- Prohibits benami transactions (i.e., properties bought in the name of another person to hide ownership).
- Allows the government to seize such properties.

7. Foreign Exchange Management Act (FEMA), 1999

FEMA regulates foreign investments in Indian real estate and ensures that foreign exchange transactions comply with the laws of India. Non-resident Indians (NRIs) and Persons of Indian Origin (PIOs) can buy property in India under certain conditions set by FEMA.

Key Provisions:

- NRIs can buy residential and commercial property without any special permissions.

- Restrictions apply to the purchase of agricultural land, farmhouses, and plantation properties.
- FEMA works alongside RERA to ensure that foreign buyers follow legal guidelines in real estate transactions. If there is a violation of foreign exchange regulations, FEMA will override RERA in terms of penalties or legal actions for foreign buyers.

Which Law Prevails?

- For project completion and transparency issues, RERA will prevail over older laws like MOFA or MAOA.
- In case of consumer grievances related to service deficiencies, buyers can still approach forums under the Consumer Protection Act, but RERA remains the primary recourse for real estate-related matters.
- In case of insolvency of a developer, IBC will take precedence, but buyers will still be treated as creditors.
- For issues like money laundering, benami transactions, or foreign exchange violations, respective laws like PMLA, Benami Act, or FEMA will override RERA.

For Maharashtra, RERA marks a critical shift towards a more buyer-centric real estate market. It harmonizes the various legal provisions, ensuring transparency, timely completion, and protection of homebuyers' rights, making it a significant improvement over previous law like MOFA and MAOA.

Chapter 4

Constitutional Validity of RERA

The constitutional validity of RERA was challenged in the case of Neelkamal Realtors Suburban Pvt. Ltd. & Ors. v. Union of India & Ors. This landmark case, decided by the Bombay High Court in 2017, tested whether RERA was constitutionally sound and fair to all parties involved, particularly the builders and developers.

Key Issues in the Case:

Neelkamal Realtors and other developers argued that RERA was unconstitutional on several grounds:

1. Retrospective Application of RERA: The petitioners argued that RERA's provisions applied to ongoing projects, i.e., projects that had commenced before the Act came into force. They claimed that this retrospective application placed undue hardship on builders, forcing them to comply with new standards for projects already underway.
2. Violation of Article 14 (Right to Equality): The developers contended that RERA discriminated against builders by imposing stringent regulations on them while protecting homebuyers. They argued that this unequal treatment violated Article 14 of the Constitution, which guarantees equality before the law.
3. Violation of Article 19(1)(g) (Right to Freedom of Trade): It was argued that RERA violated the right to practice any profession or trade by placing excessive restrictions on developers, thus infringing upon their fundamental rights under Article 19(1)(g).
4. Excessive Regulation: The developers claimed that RERA's provisions—such as requiring developers to deposit 70% of project funds in an escrow account and providing compensation to buyers for delays—were too onerous and interfered with their business operations.

Key Findings of the Bombay High Court:

The Bombay High Court upheld the constitutional validity of RERA and dismissed the arguments made by the petitioners. The Court's ruling was based on the following principles:

1. Retrospective Application:

- The Court found that RERA was not retrospective in nature, as it did not affect projects that were completed before the Act came into force. It only applied to ongoing projects and projects yet to be completed. The Court ruled that the legislative intent behind this was to protect homebuyers who had already invested in such projects and faced delays.
- The retrospective application to ongoing projects was found to be -reasonable and justified in the interest of protecting the rights of homebuyers.

2. Article 14 (Right to Equality):

- The Court rejected the argument that RERA discriminated against developers. It held that homebuyers and developers are not equals, and thus cannot be treated the same way under the law. The Court reasoned that the two groups have different positions and interests, and the protection offered to homebuyers under RERA was legitimate given the prevalent issues in the real estate sector, such as project delays and non-completion.
- Therefore, the classification made by RERA, providing more protection to homebuyers, was held to be reasonable and in line with Article 14 of the Constitution.

3. Article 19(1)(g) (Right to Freedom of Trade):

- The Court acknowledged that while RERA imposed certain restrictions on developers, these restrictions were reasonable and in the larger interest of the public. The objective of RERA was to ensure accountability, transparency, and efficiency in the real estate sector, which had seen frequent defaults by developers to the detriment of homebuyers.
- The Court ruled that reasonable restrictions on the freedom of trade were permissible under Article 19(6) of the Constitution,

and RERA's provisions were aimed at regulating a previously unregulated sector for the greater good.

4. Reasonableness of Regulations:
   - The Court found that the 70% escrow provision, which mandates developers to deposit 70% of the project funds into an escrow account for construction and land purposes, was a reasonable measure to ensure that the funds were not diverted to other projects.
   - The requirement of compensation for delays was also held to be fair, as it protected the homebuyers from indefinite delays in project delivery—a persistent problem in the real estate sector.

The Bombay High Court upheld the constitutional validity of RERA in its entirety. The Court emphasized that RERA was enacted to address the imbalance of power between developers and homebuyers and to bring about accountability and transparency in the real estate sector. The Court's ruling established that:

- RERA's application to ongoing projects was justified in the interest of homebuyers.
- The Act did not violate the right to equality or freedom of trade, as it imposed reasonable restrictions in the public interest.
- The overall objective of RERA—to protect homebuyers and regulate the real estate market—was constitutional and aligned with the principles of justice, equity, and good governance.

This judgment reinforced RERA as a consumer-centric law that addressed the long-standing issues faced by homebuyers and regulated the developers' responsibilities in a fair and balanced manner. The ruling also set a precedent for future legal challenges to RERA, affirming that the Act was within the constitutional framework.

Part 8
Landmark Rulings

I. Long Lease is Tantamount to Sale, thus very much under the Jurisdiction of RERA

Case No.: Second Appeal, No. 9717 of 2018

Citation: Lavasa Corporation Limited Vs. Jitendra Jagdish Tulsiani

Coram: Dr. Shalini Phansalkar-Joshi, J.

Order Date: 2018-08-07

Background

The order concerns appeal filed by Lavasa Corporation, which is developing a township project and has registered under the Real Estate (Regulation and Development) Act, 2016 (RERA). The main legal issue is whether the provisions of RERA apply to "Agreements to Lease," particularly when the lease is for a long duration (999 years) and substantial consideration has been paid.

Key Points:

1. Appellant's Argument: Lavasa argued that these agreements are leases, not sales, and therefore, RERA does not apply. They contended that since RERA is intended for sales and does not cover leases, the adjudicating authority under RERA has no jurisdiction over the complaints.
2. Adjudicating Authority's Decision: Initially, the adjudicating authority agreed with Lavasa, ruling that RERA does not apply to leases, and therefore, it dismissed the complaints due to lack of jurisdiction.
3. Appellate Tribunal's Decision: The Respondents appealed, and the Appellate Tribunal reversed the decision, stating that the lease agreements, in essence, functioned as sales agreements. The Tribunal held that since Lavasa registered under RERA, it cannot now claim that RERA does not apply. It invoked the principle of estoppel under Section 115 of the Indian Evidence Act, preventing Lavasa from denying the jurisdiction of RERA.

4. Appeal to Higher Court: Lavasa challenged the Tribunal's decision, arguing that the agreements were clearly for lease and not for sale, and thus RERA does not apply. They also argued that merely registering under RERA should not automatically bring lease agreements under its purview.
5. Respondent's Argument: The Respondents argued that the lease agreements were essentially sales, given the long duration and substantial payments made. They asserted that RERA applies because the agreement was more about transferring ownership, despite being labelled as a lease.
6. Current Status: The matter is under appeal, and the key issue remains whether the RERA provisions should apply to these long-term lease agreements, which are essentially akin to sales.

II. RERA has no Jurisdiction on Industrial Units

Case No.: 158/2023

Citation: Inspira Realty vs Maha RERA

Order Date: August 12, 2023

Background:

On April 26, 2023, the Maharashtra Real Estate Regulatory Authority (Maha RERA) delegated powers under Section 81 of the Real Estate (Regulation and Development) Act, 2016 (RERA) to the authority issuing this order, including the power to impose penalties under Sections 59 and 61 for contraventions of RERA. On August 26, 2023, advertisements were published in the Maharashtra Times and Lokmat newspapers regarding the real estate project "INSPIRA CITY SHENDRA" without registering the project with Maha RERA. A show-cause notice was issued to the Respondent-Promoter on September 13, 2023, asking why penal action under Section 59 should not be initiated.

Respondent-Promoter's Argument:

The Respondent-Promoter filed a reply on October 5, 2023, clarifying that the project is an industrial project managed by "Inspira Infra (Aurangabad) Limited" and not by "Inspira Realty LLP." The project involves industrial land leased from MIDC for 95 years to develop an Integrated Industrial Area (IIA). The Respondent argued that the RERA Act does not apply to industrial projects and cited orders from the Maha RERA Appellate Tribunal that support the exclusion of industrial projects from RERA's purview. The Respondent concluded that there was no violation of RERA and requested the withdrawal of the show-cause notice.

Hearing:

A hearing was held on October 31, 2023, with the Respondent's legal representative, Adv. Abir Patel, reiterating the arguments. He emphasized that the project is an industrial plot governed by the MIDC Act, not RERA, and pointed to previous orders by the Maha RERA Appellate Tribunal that confirmed RERA's inapplicability to industrial projects.

Previous Tribunal Rulings:

The MahaRERA Appellate Tribunal, in two appeals (Appeal No. AT006000000052195 and Appeal No. AT006000000031585), held that RERA applies only to residential and commercial projects, and industrial projects fall outside its purview. This interpretation aligns with the exclusion of industrial use from the definitions provided in RERA.

Decision:

Given that the impugned advertisement relates to an industrial plot, and considering the Respondent's arguments, the relevant legal provisions, and previous Tribunal rulings, it was concluded that the Respondent-Promoter did not violate Section 3 of RERA. Therefore, no penal action will be imposed.

III. Exemption from Registration

Case No.: Appeal SC 10000672/691

Citation: M/s Geetanjali Aman Constructions & Ors Vs Hrishikesh Ramesh Paranjpe & Ors

Coram: Indira Jain., Chairperson; Sumant Kolhe Member (J); S.S. Sandhu, Member (A)

Order Date: 2019-07-10

Section: Section 3

Background:

The appeal centres around the interpretation of Clause (a) of Section 3(2) of the Real Estate (Regulation and Development) Act, 2016 (RERA), particularly concerning the exemption of certain projects from registration based on the area of the plot or the number of apartments involved.

Legal Issue:

The key issue is whether a project that is to be developed in phases requires registration under RERA for each phase, even if the overall project might qualify for an exemption under Clause (a) of Section 3(2).

Court's Interpretation:

The court emphasized that under Section 3 of RERA, each phase of a project must be considered a standalone real estate project, requiring separate registration. The court noted that the legislative intent behind this provision is to ensure that the Regulatory Authority can effectively supervise, monitor, and control each phase of the project, thereby fulfilling the objectives of RERA.

Conclusion:

The court held that unless a project is duly registered with Maha RERA, the Regulatory Authority cannot fulfil its mandate of overseeing the project's progress. Therefore, the exemption from registration should only apply when both conditions specified in Clause (a) are satisfied. The ruling reinforces the necessity of separate registrations for each phase of a phased development project under RERA.

IV. Agricultural Land is not under RERA's Jurisdiction

Case No.: Appeal No. U-21

Citation: Mohammed Zain Khan Vs Enmoy Properties India and Ors

Coram: Indira Jain., Chairperson; S.S. Sandhu, Member (A)

Order Date: 2019-10-09

Section: Section 3

Background:

The case of Mohammed Zain Khan vs. Emnoy Properties India Private Limited is a significant one concerning the applicability of the Real Estate (Regulation and Development) Act, 2016 (RERA) to agricultural land. This case specifically dealt with whether agricultural land that was marketed for sale by a real estate developer falls under the jurisdiction of RERA.

Facts of the Case:

Plaintiff (Mohammed Zain Khan):

The plaintiff, Mohammed Zain Khan, filed a complaint with the Maharashtra Real Estate Regulatory Authority (Maha RERA) against Emnoy Properties India Pvt. Ltd., a real estate developer.

Defendant (Emnoy Properties India):

The developer, Emnoy Properties, was selling plots of agricultural land. The complaint was filed under the premise that the developer was marketing these plots under the guise of future development potential, implying that the land could be developed for residential or commercial purposes.

Key Issues:

1. Nature of the Land:

The primary issue was whether the agricultural land sold by Emnoy Properties fell under RERA's jurisdiction. The crux of the matter was whether these plots were being marketed as agricultural land or if there was an implied promise of future development, which would bring it under RERA.

2. Jurisdiction of RERA:

RERA's jurisdiction typically covers projects that involve the development of land for the construction of buildings or the sale of developed plots intended for residential, commercial, or industrial use. The question here was whether mere agricultural land, without any approved development plans, could be considered a "real estate project" under RERA.

Maha RERA's Decision:

- The Maha RERA Authority ruled in favour of Emnoy Properties. It was determined that since the plots in question were classified as agricultural land and were sold as such, without any approved plan for conversion to non-agricultural use, the transaction did not fall within RERA's purview.

The authority clarified that RERA regulates only those projects where there is an intention to develop the land for construction or sell developed plots. Since Emnoy Properties was selling the plots as agricultural land, with no immediate or approved plans for development, it was outside RERA's jurisdiction.

Conclusion:

The case between Mohammed Zain Khan and Emnoy Properties India Pvt. Ltd. highlighted the limitations of RERA's jurisdiction concerning agricultural land. It established that unless agricultural land is intended for development into a real estate project, it does not fall under RERA's ambit. This case serves as a crucial reference for understanding how RERA applies (or doesn't apply) to transactions involving agricultural land in India.

V. One Registration per Project

Case No.: CC006000000000345

Citation: Kishor Jadha Vs Jayantibai Patel and Ors

Coram: Hon'ble Shri Goulom Chollerjee, Chairperson; Hon'ble Br. Vijay Satbir Singh, Member 1

Order Date: 2019-09-19

Section: Section 4

Background:

In this case, the dispute arose when two separate registrations were sought for what was essentially the same real estate project. Kishor Jadha, the complainant, argued that the project had already been registered under RERA by another entity, and therefore, a second registration by Jayantibai Patel (the respondent) was unnecessary and illegal.

Facts of the Case:

- The real estate project in question was initially registered under RERA by one entity, which had completed certain formalities and begun work on the project.
- Subsequently, a second registration was filed by Jayantibai Patel, claiming authority over the same project.
- Kishor Jadha filed a complaint, arguing that RERA does not allow multiple registrations for the same project as it would lead to confusion and potential exploitation of buyers.

Respondent's Argument:

Jayantibai Patel argued that the second registration was necessary due to changes in the project's development plans and the involvement of new stakeholders. The respondent claimed that this second registration was in line with the evolving nature of the project and did not intend to deceive or mislead buyers.

Key Legal Issues:

1. Multiple Registrations: The primary issue was whether RERA permits more than one registration for the same project. The law aims to bring transparency and clarity to real estate transactions, and multiple registrations could undermine these objectives.
2. Impact on Buyers: Multiple registrations could lead to confusion among buyers regarding the project's legitimacy, ownership, and the entity responsible for completing the project.

RERA's Ruling:

- Single Registration Rule: The RERA Authority ruled that no two registrations can be allowed for the same real estate project. The intention behind RERA is to ensure transparency, protect the interests of homebuyers, and prevent any ambiguity regarding the project's status.
- Clarity and Transparency: The ruling emphasized that allowing multiple registrations could result in a lack of clarity and transparency, which RERA seeks to avoid. The RERA Act mandates that all details about a project, including ownership, development plans, and timelines, be clearly disclosed to buyers under a single registration.
- Cancellation of Second Registration: The Authority ordered the cancellation of the second registration filed by Jayantibai Patel, reaffirming that the original registration by the first entity was valid and that all further activities related to the project should be conducted under that registration.

Conclusion:

The ruling in the case between Kishor Jadha and Jayantibai Patel highlights the importance of maintaining a single registration for a real estate project under RERA. This ensures transparency, clarity, and protection for all stakeholders involved, particularly homebuyers. The decision to cancel the second registration reaffirms RERA's commitment to these principles.

VI. Grace Period above Date of Possession is not Accepted

Case No.: Second Appeal No. 5329 of 2020

Citation: Westin Developers Pvt. Ltd. Vs Raymond Alexis

Coram: S.C. Gupte J

Order Date: 2020-12-04

Section: Section 18

Background:

The dispute between Westin Developers Pvt. Ltd. (the developer) and Raymond Alexis (the complainant) cantered on the delayed possession of a property. The complainant had booked a flat in a project developed by Westin Developers, with a specified possession date mentioned in the agreement. The developer, however, delayed handing over the possession, citing a "grace period" clause that they argued allowed them additional time beyond the agreed possession date.

Facts of the Case:

- Raymond Alexis had entered into an agreement with Westin Developers for the purchase of a flat, with a clearly stipulated possession date.
- Westin Developers failed to deliver the possession by the agreed date and invoked a "grace period" clause in the agreement, claiming that they were entitled to an additional period beyond the possession date to complete the project without facing penalties.
- Raymond Alexis filed a complaint with the Real Estate Regulatory Authority (RERA), arguing that the developer's invocation of the grace period was unjustified and that he was entitled to compensation for the delay.

Respondent-Developer's Argument:

- Westin Developers argued that the grace period clause was a standard provision in the agreement, intended to account for unforeseen delays in construction or regulatory approvals.
- They contended that the clause was legal and enforceable, allowing them additional time to complete the project without penalty.

Key Legal Issues:

1. Validity of Grace Period Clauses: The central issue was whether a developer could unilaterally extend the possession date by invoking a grace period clause, especially when such a delay would adversely affect the buyer.
2. Homebuyer Rights under RERA: The case also touched upon the rights of homebuyers under RERA, particularly regarding timely possession and the consequences of delays by developers.

RERA's Ruling:

- Non-Acceptance of Grace Period Beyond Possession Date: The RERA Authority ruled that grace period clauses, which allow developers to extend the possession date without penalty, are not acceptable if they cause undue delay and inconvenience to the homebuyer. RERA's primary objective is to protect the interests of homebuyers, ensuring timely delivery of possession.
- Strict Adherence to Possession Dates: The ruling emphasized that developers must adhere strictly to the possession dates mentioned in the agreement. Any delay beyond this date, without justifiable cause, would attract penalties, including the obligation to pay interest or compensation to the buyer.
- Invalidation of Grace Period Clause: In this particular case, RERA invalidated the grace period clause invoked by Westin Developers, stating that it could not be used as an excuse to delay possession indefinitely. The developer was held liable for the delay and was directed to compensate Raymond Alexis accordingly.

Conclusion:

The judgment in the case between Westin Developers Pvt. Ltd. and Raymond Alexis clarifies that grace period clauses cannot be used by developers as a blanket excuse for delaying possession beyond the agreed date. RERA prioritizes the timely delivery of properties to homebuyers, and any attempt to delay possession unjustly will result in penalties and compensation to the affected buyers. This ruling strengthens the protection of homebuyers under RERA, ensuring they receive their properties as promised.

VII. Allotment Letters are Agreements

Case No.: AT006000000010977

Citation: Mrs. Amrita Kaur and Ors Vs. East & West Builders

Coram: S.M. Kolhe, Member (J), S.S. Sandhu, Member (A)

Order Date: 2020-02-20

Section: Section 18

Background:

The case revolves around a dispute between Mrs. Amrita Kaur & Ors (the complainants) and M/s. East and West Builders (the developer) regarding the delayed possession of flats booked by the complainants. The complainants argued that the developer had failed to deliver possession within the agreed-upon timeline, which led to filing a complaint under the Real Estate Regulatory Authority (RERA). The developer defended themselves by relying on the allotment letter issued to the complainants.

Facts of the Case:

- The complainants had booked flats in a project being developed by M/s. East and West Builders and were issued allotment letters by the developer. However, the developer failed to adhere to the specified possession timeline.
- The developer contended that the allotment letter, which did not explicitly specify the possession date, acted as an agreement, and they were not obligated to deliver the property within a fixed timeline.
- The complainants, however, argued that they were entitled to compensation for the delayed possession, citing the terms of the agreement which the developer had not honoured.

Respondent-Developer's Argument:

- The developer claimed that the allotment letter should be treated as a binding agreement between the parties. They contended that the allotment letter contained the relevant terms of the transaction and that they were not in breach of any legal obligation as the letter did not define a strict possession date.

Key Legal Issues:

1. Can an Allotment Letter be Considered a Binding Agreement?

The core issue was whether an allotment letter, which lacked a specific possession date and was not registered, could be regarded as an enforceable legal document under RERA.

2. Homebuyer Rights under RERA: The case also dealt with the rights of homebuyers concerning timely possession and the legal validity of the documents provided by the developer.

RERA's Ruling:

- Allotment Letters are Not Binding Agreements: The RERA Authority ruled that an allotment letter cannot be treated as a legally enforceable agreement for sale unless it conforms to the requirements of the Real Estate (Regulation and Development) Act, 2016 (RERA). The authority emphasized that the letter lacked crucial elements, such as a specified possession date and registration, which are mandatory under RERA for an agreement to be binding.
- Requirement for a Registered Agreement for Sale: The judgment reinforced the fact that only a registered agreement for sale, which includes essential details like the possession date and is executed in accordance with RERA guidelines, can be treated as binding. Any delay beyond the possession date mentioned in such an agreement would entitle the buyer to compensation.
- Developer's Liability for Delayed Possession: In this case, the developer was found liable for the delay, and the allotment letter could not shield them from their responsibility to deliver possession within a reasonable timeframe.

Conclusion:

In the case between Mrs. Amrita Kaur & Ors vs. M/s. East and West Builders, Maha RERA ruled that an allotment letter, without a proper agreement for sale, cannot be considered a legally binding document. The ruling reinforced the importance of developers adhering to possession timelines mentioned in registered agreements, and the developer was held accountable for the delay, providing much-needed clarity on homebuyer rights under RERA.

VIII. Part OC is not Accepted

Case No.: AT006000000010979

Citation: Rajesh B. Dhume Vs Lucina Land Development Ltd.

Coram: Indira Jain., Chairperson; S.S. Sandhu, Member (A)

Order Date: 2021-09-17

Section: Section 18

Background:

Rajesh B. Dhume and other homebuyers booked flats in Indiabulls Park 2, a project by Lucina Land Development Ltd. The developer had promised possession by November 2020. However, due to construction delays, the buyers did not receive possession as per the agreement, which led them to file a complaint with MahaRERA, seeking compensation for the delay.

Facts of the Case:

- The homebuyers entered into agreements with the developer for the purchase of flats, with a possession date set for November 2020.
- The developer claimed that the delay was due to unforeseen circumstances, including COVID-19, and extended the possession deadline first to August 2021 and then to June 2023.
- Rajesh B. Dhume and other buyers contended that the developer was already behind schedule even before the pandemic, and further extensions were unacceptable. They sought compensation in the form of interest for the delayed possession.

Respondent-Developer's Argument:

- Lucina Land Development argued that the delays were caused by reasons beyond their control, including the impact of the COVID-19 pandemic.

- They pointed to a grace period clause in the agreement and claimed that Maha RERA had allowed for an extension in the possession timeline due to the pandemic, pushing the date to June 2023.

Key Legal Issues:

1. Validity of the Grace Period and Extensions: Could the developer lawfully extend the possession date by invoking grace period clauses and force majeure due to COVID-19?
2. Homebuyer Rights under RERA: Were the homebuyers entitled to compensation for the delay, despite the developer's claims of extensions?

RERA's Ruling:

Grace Period and Delays: Maha RERA ruled that while certain delays due to force majeure (like the pandemic) may be acceptable, the developer had already extended possession beyond a reasonable period before the pandemic.

Compensation for Delayed Possession: Under Section 18 of RERA, the authority held that the homebuyers were entitled to compensation. The developer was directed to pay interest from February 2022 until the actual handover of possession for the undue delay in completing the project.

Conclusion:

In the case between Rajesh B. Dhume vs. Lucina Land Development Ltd., Maha RERA ruled that the developer was liable for delays and directed them to compensate the homebuyers with interest. The ruling highlights that developers must provide possession within a reasonable period and cannot indefinitely extend deadlines under grace periods or force majeure clauses.

IX. A Complaint can be Filed with RERA even after the OC is Received

Case No.: AT006000000010684

Citation: Lodha Bellissimo Crown Buildmart Pvt. Ltd. Vs Haresh Jethmal Asher

Coram: Hon'ble Shri K.U. Chandiwal

Order Date: 2018-10-26

Section: Section 3,18

Background:

In the case of Lodha Bellissimo Crown Buildmart Pvt Ltd vs. Haresh Jethmal Asher, the dispute arose over whether a complaint could be filed with RERA after the receipt of the Occupancy Certificate (OC). Haresh Asher, the complainant, had grievances regarding delayed possession and issues with amenities, despite the project having received its OC.

Facts of the Case:

- Haresh Jethmal Asher purchased a flat in a project by Lodha Bellissimo Crown Buildmart Pvt Ltd.
- The builder had obtained an OC, but the complainant argued that there were deficiencies in the promised amenities and that possession was delayed.
- Asher filed a complaint with Maha RERA, challenging the developer's failure to fulfil commitments, despite the issuance of the OC.

Respondent's Argument:

- Lodha Bellissimo contended that since they had received the OC, Maha RERA had no jurisdiction to entertain the complaint. They argued that the OC signified the project's completion, and any complaints after this point should not be heard by RERA.

Key Legal Issues:

1. Post-OC Complaints: The central issue was whether RERA could still entertain complaints after an OC was granted.
2. Homebuyer Rights Under RERA Post-OC: The case examined the continuing rights of homebuyers to seek redress under RERA even after an OC is obtained.

RERA's Ruling:

- Acceptance of Complaints Post-OC: MahaRERA ruled that a complaint can indeed be filed after the issuance of the OC if the homebuyer faces issues like non-compliance with the agreement, lack of promised amenities, or delayed possession. The authority noted that receiving an OC does not absolve the developer of responsibilities under RERA.
- Jurisdiction of RERA Post-OC: RERA emphasized that it retains jurisdiction over the project even after an OC is issued. This protects homebuyers' rights, ensuring they receive the amenities and quality promised in their agreements, not just the physical possession of the property.

Conclusion:

In the Lodha Bellissimo vs. Haresh Jethmal Asher case, RERA clarified that the issuance of an OC does not bar complaints under RERA. The developer is still accountable for the timely possession and delivery of all promised amenities, ensuring greater protection for homebuyers.

X. An OC Cannot be Complete Without a Water Connection and Working Lifts

Case No.: Writ Petition (L) No. 21683 of 2022

Citation: Subodh M. Joshi Vs MCGM

Coram: G.S. Patel & Gauri Godse, JJ.

Order Date: 2022-08-17

Section: Section 2

Background:

- Subodh Joshi, the petitioner, was allocated a flat as part of a rehabilitation project. The flat in question, C-501, was in a building claimed by the developer to be "ready for occupation."
- However, Joshi highlighted several concerns, notably that the building lacked a drinking water connection and fully operational lifts. Despite these deficiencies, the Municipal Corporation of Greater Mumbai (MCGM) had issued an OC for the building, allowing people to move in.
- Joshi argued that without these essential amenities, the building was not fit for habitation.

Key Legal Issues:

1. Validity of OC without Water Supply and Lifts: The primary legal question was whether an OC could be considered valid when a building lacked critical infrastructure like drinking water and functioning lifts.
2. Responsibility of Developers and Civic Authorities: The case also examined the obligations of both the developer and the municipal authority in ensuring that basic amenities are in place before an OC is granted.

RERA's Ruling:

- OC Without Water and Functional Lifts is Incomplete: The court ruled that an OC cannot be considered valid if essential services like drinking water and operational lifts are not provided. These services are fundamental for making a building habitable, and issuing an OC without them undermines the safety and well-being of residents.
- Developer Accountability: The court emphasized that developers must plan ahead to ensure that all necessary infrastructure is in place before seeking an OC. The developer's failure to secure a water connection in a timely manner was deemed unacceptable.
- Municipal Corporation's Role: The Municipal Corporation was also criticized for issuing an OC without verifying the completion of these essential services. The court warned that it would closely scrutinize such practices in future cases to ensure residents' rights are protected.

This case sets a clear precedent that OCs must reflect the true readiness of a building, focusing on the well-being and safety of its residents.

XI. Allottees are Liable to Make Payments On Time

Case No.: CC006000000196135

Citation: M/s. Keystone Realtors Pvt. Ltd Vs Mr. Sonal Tejas Shah

Coram: Dr. Vijay Satbir Singh, Hon'ble Member, Maha RERA

Order Date: 2021-09-30

Section: Section 19

Background:

The case centres around a dispute between M/s Keystone Realtors Pvt Ltd (the developer) and Mr. Sonal Tejas Shah (the allottee) over the non-payment of dues as per the terms of their agreement. Keystone Realtors filed a complaint stating that Shah had failed to make payments despite the terms outlined in the sale agreement.

Facts of the Case:

- Mr. Sonal Tejas Shah had entered into an agreement with Keystone Realtors for a property purchase.
- The developer claimed that Shah defaulted on payments, and thus the complaint was filed seeking compliance with the payment terms.
- Shah argued that delays in possession and other project-related issues affected his payment schedule.

Arguments from Both Parties:

- Developer's Argument: M/s Keystone Realtors argued that Shah was contractually obligated to make payments as per the agreed terms, regardless of the external issues that he raised.
- Allottee's Argument: Shah countered that certain delays and quality issues in the project affected his willingness to continue payments according to the pre-determined schedule.

Legal Issue:

The key issue was whether the allottee was liable to make payments in strict accordance with the terms of the agreement, even in the face of alleged delays by the developer.

RERA Ruling:

- The RERA authority ruled in favor of the developer, emphasizing that the terms of the agreement between the parties are legally binding.
- The ruling stressed that allottees are required to fulfill their payment obligations as stipulated, unless there is a significant breach by the developer that has been proven.
- In this case, Shah was held liable for making payments in line with the contractual terms.

Conclusion:

This ruling in favour of M/s Keystone Realtors highlights that the terms and conditions of agreements are binding, and allottees must meet their payment schedules unless they can demonstrate that the developer has significantly defaulted on their obligations.

XII. Pre-Deposit is Mandatory

Case No.: MA 469/20 in ATOO6O00000052775

Citation: Avarsekar Realty Pvt. Ltd Vs Ashok Pranjpe

Coram: Sumant M. Kohle, Member, S.S. Sandhu, Member

Order Date: 2021-05-21

Section: Section 43

Background:

The case centres on Avarsekar Realty Pvt Ltd (the developer) and Ashok Paranjpe & Anr. (the allottees) concerning a dispute over compensation awarded by an adjudicating officer. The developer sought to file an appeal without the pre-deposit mandated under RERA.

Facts of the Case:

- The adjudicating officer ordered compensation to the allottees for delays in possession.
- Avarsekar Realty attempted to appeal the order without making the mandatory pre-deposit, as required under Section 43(5) of the Real Estate (Regulation and Development) Act (RERA).

Developer's Argument:

The developer contended that the pre-deposit should not apply because the order was passed by an adjudicating officer and not the RERA Authority.

Key Legal Issue:

The primary legal issue was whether the pre-deposit requirement is mandatory even when an order is passed by an adjudicating officer, as opposed to the RERA Authority.

RERA's Ruling:

- The RERA Appellate Tribunal ruled that *the pre-deposit is mandatory for filing an appeal*, even if the original order is passed by an adjudicating officer.
- The Tribunal emphasized that the intent of RERA is to ensure that compensation awarded to homebuyers is not delayed by protracted legal processes.
- As a result, Avarsekar Realty was required to make the pre-deposit before proceeding with the appeal.

Conclusion:

The ruling in the case between Avarsekar Realty Pvt Ltd and Ashok Paranjpe establishes that the pre-deposit is a mandatory requirement for filing appeals under RERA, regardless of whether the order is issued by an adjudicating officer or the RERA Authority. This ensures that homebuyers' claims for compensation are upheld and not delayed by unnecessary legal appeals.

XIII. Authority is under an Obligation to Complete a Revoked Project

Case No.: CC006000000120981

Citation: Mithanagar Archana CHS ltd VS Dhanashree Developers Pvt ltd

Coram: Shri Ajoy Mehta, Chairman

Order Date: 2022-10-21

Section: Section 7,8,15

Background:

This case concerns a dispute between Mithanagar Archana CHS Ltd (the society) and Dhanashree Developers Pvt Ltd (the developer) regarding the failure to complete a redevelopment project in Goregaon, Mumbai. The developer's registration was revoked under the Real Estate (Regulation and Development) Act (RERA) due to project delays and financial difficulties.

Facts of the Case:

Mithanagar Archana CHS Ltd had entered into a redevelopment agreement with Dhanashree Developers for reconstructing its housing society.

The project was significantly delayed, and the developer failed to renew its registration after its expiration.

Dhanashree Developers faced financial and legal difficulties, including a winding-up order from the Bombay High Court.

The society, representing 36 members, filed a complaint with MahaRERA, seeking to revoke the developer's registration and appoint a new developer to complete the project.

Arguments from Both Parties:

Developer's Argument: Dhanashree Developers requested that it be allowed to continue the project under Section 7(3) of RERA, despite the expiration of its registration, arguing that it could still complete the remaining work.

Society's Argument: The society argued that the developer was no longer capable of completing the project due to financial challenges and delays, and requested MahaRERA to intervene and appoint a new developer.

Key Legal Issue:

The key issue was whether RERA is obligated to take steps to ensure the completion of the remaining development work in a project after the developer's registration has been revoked.

RERA's Ruling:

Obligation to Ensure Completion of the Project: MahaRERA ruled that the authority is under an obligation to ensure that the remaining development work in a project, where the developer's registration has been revoked, is completed.

Sections 7 and 8 of RERA Invoked: Under Sections 7 and 8, MahaRERA revoked the developer's registration and initiated steps to facilitate the project's completion by a new developer or through a resolution by the society members.

Stakeholder Involvement: Maha RERA directed the society to hold a meeting with stakeholders, including the affected allottees and the new developer, to discuss the completion of the project.

Conclusion:

The ruling in the case of Mithanagar Archana CHS Ltd vs Dhanashree Developers Pvt Ltd establishes that Maha RERA must ensure that the balance development work is completed when a project has been revoked. The ruling protects homebuyers' interests by mandating the involvement of stakeholders and taking steps to ensure that redevelopment projects are not abandoned due to a developer's failure.

XIV. 3 Years is Sufficient for Possession

Case No.: AT006000000052806

Citation: Mr. Ishaque Qasimali Shaikh Vs. M/s. Jangid Properties

Coram: Indira Jain J., Chairperson & K. Shivaji

Order Date: 2022-03-10

Section: Section 13,18

Background:

The dispute involved Mr. Ishaque Qasimali Shaikh, who booked a flat in the Jangid Enclave project by M/s Jangid Properties. While the allotment and sale agreement were signed, no specific possession date was mentioned. Mr. Shaikh contended that the developer had verbally promised possession by April 2014, but it was delayed beyond that.

Facts of the Case:

The allotment letter was issued in October 2012, and the sale agreement was executed in June 2013, but no possession date was mentioned.

Mr. Shaikh claimed the developer verbally promised possession by April 2014, but after multiple revisions, the possession date was pushed to October 2020.

In November 2019, Mr. Shaikh filed a complaint with MahaRERA seeking interest for the delay in possession from the verbally promised date of April 2014.

Respondent-Developer's Argument:

M/s Jangid Properties argued that since no possession date was mentioned in the agreement, the revised possession dates mentioned during the RERA registration should be considered valid.

They contended that they were entitled to additional time due to unforeseen construction delays and that Mr. Shaikh should have pursued earlier legal remedies under the Maharashtra Ownership of Flats Act (MOFA).

Key Legal Issues:

Possession Date in Absence of Agreement Terms: Whether a reasonable possession timeline can be determined when no specific date is mentioned in the agreement for sale.

Rights of Homebuyers: The case examined the developer's liability under both MOFA and RERA and the homebuyer's rights to compensation for delayed possession.

RERA's Ruling:

Three Years Sufficient for Delivery: The RERA Appellate Tribunal ruled that even if no possession date is specified in the agreement, three years from the date of the sale agreement is considered a reasonable period for delivery.

Rejection of Revised Dates: The Tribunal also noted that unilaterally revising the possession date during the RERA registration process without the buyer's consent is not legally binding.

Interest for Delay: M/s Jangid Properties was ordered to pay interest on the delayed possession from June 28, 2016 (three years after the sale agreement was signed) until possession is granted.

Conclusion:

The ruling in the case between Mr. Ishaque Qasimali Shaikh and M/s Jangid Properties confirms that even when a possession date is missing in the agreement, a three-year period is reasonable for completion. Developers cannot unilaterally extend possession timelines, and delays beyond this period without consent will attract penalties, including interest for the homebuyer.

XV. A Promoter can Advertise his Project Without Registration

Case No.: Appeal no. 164/2019

Citation: M/S Shri Ram Corporation Vs Gujarat Real Estate Appellate Tribunal

Coram: R.N. Dave

Order Date: 2020-01-17

Section: Section 44

Background:

The dispute involved M/s Shri Ram Corporation, a promoter, and the Gujarat Real Estate Appellate Tribunal, concerning the advertisement of a real estate project without proper RERA registration.

Facts of the Case:

M/s Shri Ram Corporation had launched an advertisement for their project but had not registered the project with RERA as required under the Real Estate (Regulation and Development) Act, 2016.

Gujarat Real Estate Regulatory Authority (GujRERA) took note of the violation and imposed penalties on the promoter for advertising an unregistered project.

M/s Shri Ram Corporation challenged the decision, arguing that registration was unnecessary as the project was still in its initial planning phase.

Respondent-Developer's Argument:

The promoter argued that their project was not fully underway, and since they were only in the early stages of development, they believed that RERA registration was premature.

They contended that no actual construction had begun, and thus, the advertisement did not fall under the requirement for registration.

Key Legal Issues:

1. Advertising without Registration: The main issue was whether a promoter can advertise a real estate project without completing RERA registration.
2. Definition of "Project" under RERA: Clarification of what constitutes a "project" under RERA for registration purposes was a focal point in determining whether advertising a non-registered project violates the Act.

RERA's Ruling:

Mandatory Registration Before Advertisement: RERA ruled that no promoter can advertise, market, or offer a project for sale without registering it under RERA. The Act specifically prohibits any form of promotion, including advertisements, without prior registration.

Penalty for Non-Compliance: The ruling upheld the penalty imposed on M/s Shri Ram Corporation, reaffirming that any advertisement without registration violates RERA, regardless of the project's development stage.

Strict Interpretation of RERA: The judgment emphasized that RERA's provisions are clear and mandatory, aiming to protect consumers and ensure transparency. Promoters must follow all legal processes before initiating any public communication about a project.

Conclusion:

The ruling in the case between M/s Shri Ram Corporation and Gujarat Real Estate Appellate Tribunal clarified that no promoter can advertise a project without prior registration under RERA. This decision reinforces the need for compliance with the law, protecting homebuyers from being misled by unregistered projects.

XV. A Promoter can Advertise his Project Without Registration

Case No.: Appeal no. 164/2019

Citation: M/S Shri Ram Corporation Vs Gujarat Real Estate Appellate Tribunal

Coram: R.N. Dave

Order Date: 2020-01-17

Section: Section 44

Background:

The dispute involved M/s Shri Ram Corporation, a promoter, and the Gujarat Real Estate Appellate Tribunal, concerning the advertisement of a real estate project without proper RERA registration.

Facts of the Case:

M/s Shri Ram Corporation had launched an advertisement for their project but had not registered the project with RERA as required under the Real Estate (Regulation and Development) Act, 2016.

Gujarat Real Estate Regulatory Authority took note of the violation and imposed penalties on the promoter for advertising an unregistered project.

M/s Shri Ram Corporation challenged the decision, arguing that registration was unnecessary as the project was still in its initial planning phase.

Respondent-Developer's Argument:

The promoter argued that their project was not fully underway, and since they were only in the early stages of development, they believed that RERA registration was premature.

They contended that no actual construction had begun, and thus, the advertisement did not fall under the requirement for registration.

Key Legal Issues:

Advertising without Registration: The main issue was whether a promoter can advertise a real estate project without completing RERA registration.

Definition of "Project" under RERA: Clarification of what constitutes a "project" under RERA for registration purposes was a focal point in determining whether advertising a non-registered project violates the Act.

RERA's Ruling:

Mandatory Registration Before Advertisement: RERA ruled that no promoter can advertise, market, or offer a project for sale without registering it under RERA. The Act specifically prohibits any form of promotion, including advertisements, without prior registration.

Penalty for Non-Compliance: The ruling upheld the penalty imposed on M/s Shri Ram Corporation, reaffirming that any advertisement without registration violates RERA, regardless of the project's development stage.

Strict Interpretation of RERA: The judgment emphasized that RERA's provisions are clear and mandatory, aiming to protect consumers and ensure transparency. Promoters must follow all legal processes before initiating any public communication about a project.

Conclusion:

The ruling in the case between M/s Shri Ram Corporation and Gujarat Real Estate Appellate Tribunal clarified that no promoter can advertise a project without prior registration under RERA. This decision reinforces the need for compliance with the law, protecting homebuyers from being misled by unregistered projects.

XVI. An Agreement for Long Lease is Enforceable under RERA

Case No.: Appeal no. AT004000000052893

Citation: Nagpur Integrated Township Pvt. Ltd Vs Sujit Gokul Chandankhede

Coram: Sumant Kohle, Member, S.S. Sandhu, Member

Order Date: 2021-07-28

Section: Section 13

Background:

The dispute in this case involved Nagpur Integrated Township Pvt. Ltd., a developer, and Sujit Gokul Chadankhede, the complainant. The central issue was whether a long-term lease agreement falls under RERA's jurisdiction and is enforceable under the Act.

Facts of the Case:

Sujit Gokul Chadankhede had entered into a long-term lease agreement with Nagpur Integrated Township Pvt. Ltd. for a unit in their township project.

The complainant argued that the developer had delayed delivering possession of the leased property and filed a complaint with RERA, seeking relief under the Act.

The developer contended that the agreement was a long-term lease, not a sale, and thus did not fall under the purview of RERA, which primarily regulates the sale of immovable property.

Respondent-Developer's Argument:

The developer argued that RERA only applies to agreements for sale and purchase of real estate and not to lease agreements.

They further contended that a long-term lease does not constitute a "sale" under RERA's definitions, and hence, RERA has no jurisdiction over the dispute.

Key Legal Issues:

Applicability of RERA to Lease Agreements: The main issue was whether an agreement for a long-term lease could be considered enforceable under RERA and whether such transactions fell within the scope of the Act.

Definition of "Sale" under RERA: The Tribunal needed to clarify whether long-term lease agreements could be equated to sale transactions under the provisions of RERA.

RERA's Ruling:

Lease Agreements Under RERA: The Tribunal ruled that long-term lease agreements could indeed fall within the scope of RERA if the lease was for a long duration and the lessee enjoyed ownership-like rights over the property. The intention behind the transaction, rather than the legal terminology, determines RERA's applicability.

Enforceability of Lease Agreements: The Tribunal concluded that the agreement between the parties was enforceable under RERA, as it involved the right to occupy and enjoy the property for an extended period, similar to a sale transaction.

Developer's Obligations: The ruling reinforced that developers are accountable under RERA for delays or defaults in delivering possession, regardless of whether the agreement is termed as a "sale" or a "lease."

Conclusion:

The ruling in the case between Nagpur Integrated Township Pvt. Ltd. and Sujit Gokul Chadankhede clarified that long-term lease agreements can be enforceable under RERA if the lessee is granted ownership-like rights. This decision ensures that lessees are protected under RERA's provisions and that developers cannot escape accountability by categorizing transactions as leases instead of sales.

XVII. Adjudication Officer can Adjudge only Compensation

Case No.: Appeal no. AT006000000021277

Citation: Mr. Rajeev Duniyaram Singh Vs Shivshankar Builders & Developers

Coram: Sumant Kohle, Member, S.S. Sandhu, Member

Order Date: 2021-02-24

Section: Section 18

Background:

The dispute involved multiple homebuyers led by Mr. Rajeev Duniyaram Singh, who filed a complaint seeking compensation from Shivshankar Builders and Developers for delays in possession and other grievances under RERA.

Facts of the Case:

Mr. Rajeev Singh and other homebuyers booked units in the project developed by Shivshankar Builders and Developers. They were promised timely possession, but the developer failed to deliver as per the agreed timelines.

The homebuyers approached RERA, seeking compensation for the delays and for being deprived of the use of their flats.

The developer argued that only the RERA Authority has the power to adjudicate over issues of possession, while the adjudicating officer could only decide on compensation.

Respondent-Developer's Argument:

Shivshankar Builders contended that RERA separates the powers of the RERA Authority and the adjudicating officer. They argued that the adjudicating officer does not have the jurisdiction to address other reliefs like possession or cancellation, only compensation.

Key Legal Issues:

Scope of the Adjudicating Officer's Powers: Can the adjudicating officer under RERA adjudge only compensation, or does their jurisdiction extend to other forms of relief?

Right to Compensation: Determining if the homebuyers are entitled to compensation based on the delay caused by the developer.

RERA's Ruling:

Adjudicating Officer's Powers: The Tribunal ruled that the adjudicating officer is limited to adjudicating on compensation claims under Section 71 of RERA. Other issues, such as cancellation of agreements, possession, or enforcement of obligations, fall under the jurisdiction of the RERA Authority.

Focus on Compensation: In this case, the Tribunal directed the adjudicating officer to address only the compensation claims of the complainants for delays in possession, clarifying that other reliefs needed to be filed with the RERA Authority.

Conclusion:

The ruling in the case between Mr. Rajeev Duniyaram Singh and Shivshankar Builders confirmed that the adjudicating officer under RERA is empowered only to adjudge compensation claims. Other issues such as possession, cancellation, or enforcement of obligations must be brought before the RERA Authority.

XVIII. The Promoter is Not Allowed to Escalate the Price at the Time of the Handover

Case No.: Appeal no. AT006000000031740

Citation: MHADA Vs Nikhil Margi

Coram: Indira Jain, Chairperson and S.S. Sandhu, Member

Order Date: 2021-01-29

Section: Section 44

Background:

The dispute involved MHADA (Maharashtra Housing and Area Development Authority) and Nikhil Margi, a homebuyer, regarding whether the promoter could escalate the price of the property at the time of handover, despite the initial agreement.

Facts of the Case:

Nikhil Margi had booked a unit with MHADA, and the price was agreed upon at the time of booking. However, at the time of handover, MHADA escalated the price, citing rising construction costs and other factors.

Nikhil Margi challenged this price escalation, claiming that the promoter was bound by the original agreement and that price escalation at the time of handover was unjustified.

Respondent-Developer's Argument:

MHADA argued that the escalation in price was justified due to inflation, increased construction costs, and other external factors that impacted the overall project cost.

They claimed that the original agreement allowed for price adjustments if there were cost escalations during the construction period.

Key Legal Issues:

Price Escalation Clause: Whether the promoter could escalate the price at the time of handover based on external cost factors.

Homebuyer Protection Under RERA: Determining if such a price escalation violates the rights of the homebuyer under the Real Estate (Regulation and Development) Act, 2016.

RERA's Ruling:

No Price Escalation Without Agreement: RERA ruled that unless there is a specific clause in the agreement allowing for price escalation, the promoter cannot unilaterally increase the price at the time of handover. Any price escalation must be agreed upon by both parties at the time of signing the agreement.

Protection of Homebuyers: RERA emphasized that the rights of homebuyers are paramount, and developers cannot burden buyers with unexpected price escalations at the time of possession. Promoters are required to adhere to the terms and conditions of the original agreement.

Compensation and Relief: In this case, RERA ordered MHADA to hand over the property to Nikhil Margi at the originally agreed-upon price, rejecting the developer's claim for price escalation.

Conclusion:

The ruling in the case between MHADA and Nikhil Margi clarified that a promoter cannot escalate the price at the time of handover unless it is specifically provided for in the agreement. This decision protects homebuyers from unexpected cost increases and ensures that promoters adhere to their contractual obligations.

XIX. Delay in Possession has its Consequences

Case No.: Appeal no. AT006000000021407

Citation: Mr. Suryakant Yashwant Jadhav Vs. Bellissimo Hi-rise Builders Pvt. Ltd.

Coram: Sumant M. Kohle, Member, S.S. Sandhu, Member

Order Date: 2021-01-12

Section: Section 18

Background:

This case involved Mr. Suryakant Yashwant Jadhav, a homebuyer, who filed a complaint against Bellissimo Hi-Rise Builders Pvt. Ltd. for delays in possession of his property. The complainant sought to withdraw from the project and requested compensation under RERA.

Facts of the Case

- Mr. Jadhav booked a flat in a project by Bellissimo Hi-Rise Builders and was promised possession by a specific date as per the agreement.
- However, the developer delayed the delivery of possession beyond the agreed timeline.
- Frustrated by the delay, Mr. Jadhav decided to withdraw from the project and demanded a refund along with compensation for the delay.

Key Legal Issues:

1. Right to Withdraw Due to Delay: Whether the delay in possession gives the homebuyer the right to withdraw from the project and seek a refund.
2. Right to Compensation for Delay: Whether the homebuyer is entitled to compensation for the inconvenience and financial loss caused by the delay.

RERA's Ruling:

- Right to Withdraw: The RERA Authority ruled that if there is a significant delay in possession, the homebuyer has the right to withdraw from the project. The delay in delivery breaches the terms of the agreement, which entitles the buyer to seek a refund.
- Right to Compensation: RERA further ruled that the homebuyer is entitled to compensation for the delay. The developer must compensate the buyer for the interest on the amount paid due to the delay in possession.

Conclusion:

The ruling in the case of Mr. Suryakant Yashwant Jadhav vs. Bellissimo Hi-Rise Builders Pvt. Ltd. confirms that a delay in possession allows the homebuyer to withdraw from the project and entitles them to compensation. RERA ensures that homebuyers' interests are protected in cases of delayed possession, holding developers accountable.

XX. SRA Directed to Issue an OC

Case No.: CC006000000171913

Citation: Bharti Amitkumar Lathiya Vs. M/s. Charmi Nirman

Coram: Dr. Vijay Satbir Singh

Order Date: 2020-09-11

Section: Section 19

Background:

Bharti Amitkumar Lathiya and other complainants filed a case against M/s. Charmi Nirman, the developer, concerning delays in obtaining the Occupation Certificate (OC) for a project under the Slum Rehabilitation Authority (SRA) scheme.

Facts of the Case:

- The complainants were part of a slum rehabilitation project undertaken by M/s. Charmi Nirman.
- Despite the project's completion, the developer failed to obtain the OC from the SRA, causing delays in possession and other issues for the allottees.
- The complainants approached RERA, seeking an order to direct the SRA to issue the OC promptly.

Respondent-Developer's Argument:

- M/s. Charmi Nirman argued that the delay in obtaining the OC was due to bureaucratic hurdles and factors beyond their control, as the SRA is a government body responsible for issuing OCs.

Key Legal Issues:

Developer's Responsibility for Obtaining OC: Whether the developer is responsible for ensuring the timely issuance of the OC by the SRA.

Authority's Power to Direct SRA: Whether RERA has the authority to direct the SRA, a government entity, to issue the OC for the project.

RERA's Ruling:

- Developer's Obligation: RERA ruled that the developer is obligated to take all necessary steps to ensure the timely issuance of the OC. The developer cannot absolve themselves of responsibility by blaming the delay on external entities like the SRA.
- Authority's Jurisdiction: While RERA cannot directly order the SRA, it can hold the developer accountable for delays caused by the failure to secure the OC. The developer was instructed to expedite the process of obtaining the OC from the SRA.
- Compensation for Delay: The complainants were also entitled to compensation for the delay caused by the developer's failure to obtain the OC.

Conclusion:

The ruling in the case of Bharti Amitkumar Lathiya vs. M/s. Charmi Nirman highlights the developer's responsibility to ensure timely issuance of the OC and confirms that RERA can hold the developer accountable for delays even if the OC is issued by a government authority like the SRA.

XXI. AFS Supersedes all MOUs, Allotment Letters

Case No.: Appeal No. AT001000000031507

Citation: Theme InfraProject Pvt. Ltd. Vs Mr. Jitender Shamsdasani

Coram: Sumant M. Kohle, Member, S.S. Sandhu, Member

Order Date: 2020-07-06

Section: Section 18,31

Background:

The case involved Mr. Jitender Shamdasani, a homebuyer, and Theme InfraProject Pvt. Ltd. regarding delays in possession, the impact of force majeure, and the enforceability of various agreements and allotment letters.

Facts of the Case:

- Mr. Shamdasani booked a flat with Theme InfraProject, and the developer issued an allotment letter and entered into a Memorandum of Understanding (MOU) prior to signing the Agreement for Sale (AFS).
- There were delays in handing over possession, and the developer invoked the force majeure clause, citing unforeseen circumstances to justify the delay.
- Mr. Shamdasani filed a complaint under RERA, seeking interest for the delayed possession and arguing that the AFS should override any previous MOUs or allotment letters.

Respondent-Developer's Argument:

- Theme InfraProject argued that the delay in possession was due to force majeure circumstances, which were beyond their control. They claimed that this should exempt them from paying interest to the homebuyer.

- The developer also contended that the MOU and allotment letters had binding provisions that should be considered alongside the AFS.

Key Legal Issues:

1. Force Majeure and Interest for Delay: Whether the developer can invoke the force majeure clause to avoid paying interest for the delayed possession.
2. Supremacy of Agreement for Sale: Whether the AFS supersedes all previous agreements, including MOUs and allotment letters.

RERA's Ruling:

- Interest Granted Despite Force Majeure: RERA ruled that the force majeure clause does not absolve the developer from paying interest for delays in possession. Even in force majeure situations, the developer is required to compensate the buyer for the delay unless the circumstances completely impede the progress of the project.
- AFS Supersedes MOUs and Allotment Letters: RERA further clarified that the Agreement for Sale (AFS) takes precedence over all previous MOUs and allotment letters. The terms and conditions in the AFS are legally binding, and any contradictions in earlier documents become irrelevant once the AFS is signed.

Conclusion:

The ruling in the case between Theme InfraProject Pvt. Ltd. and Mr. Jitender Shamdasani affirms that force majeure does not automatically exempt developers from paying interest for delays. Additionally, once the AFS is signed, it supersedes all prior MOUs and allotment letters, ensuring that the buyer's rights are based on the final, legally binding agreement.

XXII. If an Allottee Fails to Comply, the Agreement can be Cancelled

Case No.: Appeal No. 006000000010798

Citation: Platinum Properties Vs Ashok Tukaram Khaladkar

Coram: Sumant M. Kohle, Member,

Order Date: 2019-04-02

Section: Section 44

Background:

Platinum Properties, the developer, and Ashok Tukaram Khaladkar, the allottee, were in dispute regarding non-compliance with payment obligations under the Agreement for Sale (AFS). The developer sought to cancel the agreement and sell the flat to another buyer.

Facts of the Case:

- Ashok Tukaram Khaladkar entered into an AFS with Platinum Properties for purchasing a flat.
- The allottee failed to comply with the payment schedule stipulated in the agreement.
- The developer issued notices to the allottee, warning that failure to comply would lead to cancellation of the AFS and sale of the flat to another buyer.
- When the payments were not made, Platinum Properties sought to cancel the AFS and resell the flat, leading to the complaint under RERA.

Respondent-Developer's Argument:

- Platinum Properties argued that they had the right to cancel the AFS and sell the flat to another party if the allottee failed to fulfill their financial obligations, as outlined in the agreement.

Key Legal Issues:

Cancellation of Agreement for Sale: Whether the developer has the right to cancel the AFS if the allottee fails to make payments as per the terms of the agreement.

Right to Sell the Flat to Another Buyer: Whether the promoter can sell the flat to someone else after the cancellation of the AFS due to non-compliance by the allottee.

RERA's Ruling:

- Right to Cancel AFS for Non-Compliance: RERA ruled that the promoter has the right to cancel the AFS if the allottee fails to make the necessary payments as per the terms of the agreement. The allottee's failure to comply with the payment schedule constitutes a breach of contract, justifying cancellation.
- Right to Resell the Flat: RERA also upheld the developer's right to sell the flat to another buyer after the cancellation of the AFS. However, this must be done in compliance with applicable legal processes, ensuring that the allottee is given proper notice and opportunity to remedy the default before cancellation.

Conclusion:

The ruling in Platinum Properties vs. Ashok Tukaram Khaladkar establishes that a promoter can cancel the Agreement for Sale and resell the flat to another buyer if the allottee fails to comply with the payment terms. This decision emphasizes the importance of adhering to contractual obligations in real estate transactions.

XXIII. Agreements under MOFA are Enforceable under RERA

Case No.: Appeal No. AT006000000053623

Citation: Neelkamal Realtors Suburban Pvt Ltd Vs Mr G Satish

Coram: Shri S. Shinde & Dr. K. Shivaji

Order Date: 2023-08-31

Background:

Mr. G Satish, the complainant, entered into an agreement under MOFA with Neelkamal Realtors, and there was a dispute about whether this agreement could be enforced under RERA after the enactment of the Real Estate (Regulation and Development) Act, 2016.

Facts of the Case:

Mr. G Satish had entered into an agreement with Neelkamal Realtors Suburban Pvt. Ltd. under MOFA for the purchase of a flat.

After the enactment of RERA, the complainant sought relief under RERA for delays in possession and other grievances, questioning the enforceability of his previously registered MOFA agreement under the new regulatory framework.

Neelkamal Realtors contested the application of RERA to agreements registered under MOFA, arguing that MOFA agreements were not subject to RERA provisions.

Respondent-Developer's Argument:

Neelkamal Realtors argued that MOFA agreements predated RERA and thus should be governed solely by the provisions of MOFA. They contended that RERA could not retroactively enforce provisions on previously registered agreements under a different legal framework.

Key Legal Issues:

Applicability of RERA on MOFA Agreements: Whether agreements registered under MOFA prior to the enactment of RERA are enforceable under RERA.

Enforcement of RERA Provisions on Pre-RERA Agreements: Whether RERA provisions, including compensation for delays and possession timelines, apply to agreements that were executed before RERA came into force.

RERA's Ruling:

Applicability of RERA to MOFA Agreements: RERA ruled that agreements registered under MOFA before the enactment of RERA are enforceable under the new law. The ruling confirmed that RERA provisions apply to all ongoing and incomplete projects, including those registered under MOFA, ensuring continuity of buyer protection.

Retrospective Enforcement: RERA clarified that while it does not retroactively change the legal standing of pre-RERA agreements, any ongoing obligations, such as the delivery of possession or compensation for delays, fall within RERA's jurisdiction once the act is in force. This ruling ensures that buyers under MOFA agreements are entitled to the same protections as those under RERA.

Conclusion:

The ruling in Neelkamal Realtors Suburban Pvt. Ltd. vs. Mr. G Satish establishes that agreements registered under MOFA are enforceable under RERA. This ensures that homebuyers are protected under RERA for ongoing projects, even if they initially entered into MOFA agreements.

XXIV. Court Must Take a Decree as it Stands

Case No.: Appeal No. AT006000000134137

Citation: Madhuri Satheesh Vs M/s. Ganraj Homes LLP

Coram: Shri Ram R. Jagtap & DR. K. Shivaji

Order Date: 2023-08-22

Section: Section 18

Background:

The case involved Madhuri Satheesh, a homebuyer, and M/s Ganraj Homes LLP concerning the execution of a decree issued by a court, with questions raised about whether the executing court can challenge or alter the decree.

Facts of the Case:

- Madhuri Satheesh had secured a decree from the court concerning her rights in a property dispute with M/s Ganraj Homes LLP.
- During the execution of the decree, the developer challenged certain aspects of it, arguing that the decree should be re-evaluated or modified.
- The matter was brought before the RERA Authority for clarification on the scope of the executing court's powers.

Respondent-Developer's Argument:

M/s Ganraj Homes LLP argued that the decree needed to be reconsidered during execution, as certain conditions were allegedly unfair or unenforceable in practice.

Key Legal Issues:

1. Limitations of Executing Court: Whether the executing court has the authority to go behind the decree or if it must execute the decree as it stands.

2. Finality and Binding Nature of the Decree: Whether the decree is binding and conclusive between the parties without further modification during execution.

RERA's Ruling:

- Court Cannot Go Behind the Decree: RERA ruled that the executing court cannot alter or go behind the decree. It must execute the decree as it stands, without questioning its validity or fairness. The decree, once issued, is binding and conclusive between the parties involved in the suit.
- Finality of Decree: RERA emphasized that the decree is final and binding, and the parties must comply with its terms as decreed by the court. Any grievances or challenges to the decree must be raised during the trial phase, not during execution.

Conclusion:

The ruling in Madhuri Satheesh vs. M/s Ganraj Homes LLP clarifies that courts executing decrees must take the decree as it stands, without altering or reconsidering its terms. The decree is binding and conclusive, ensuring that all parties adhere to its stipulations during the execution phase.

XXV. Promoters Must Include Details of Amenities in the Agreement for Sale

Order No.: 57/2024

Order Date: 2024-07-30

Section: Section 18

Background:

Order No. 57/2024 issued by MahaRERA focuses on the obligations of developers concerning the provision of promised amenities in real estate projects. The order highlights the importance of delivering all amenities as committed during project registration.

Facts of the Case:

- Many developers promise specific amenities to attract buyers but fail to deliver them as per the agreement, causing grievances among homebuyers.
- The order was introduced to standardize the approach regarding the non-provision of amenities and to ensure that developers fulfill their commitments to homebuyers.

Key Legal Issues:

1. Non-Provision of Amenities: Whether developers are liable for penalties if the promised amenities are not delivered by the time of possession.
2. Transparency and Buyer Protection: How the non-delivery of amenities affects the overall protection provided to homebuyers under RERA.

RERA's Ruling:

- Mandatory Compliance: MahaRERA ruled that all amenities promised during project registration must be delivered. Failure to do so is considered a breach of contract and can result in penalties.

- No Possession Without Amenities: Developers cannot offer possession until all the promised amenities are in place or alternative arrangements are made to the buyer's satisfaction.
- Transparency in Advertising: The ruling emphasizes that developers must be clear in their project advertisements and agreement clauses about the amenities being offered.

Conclusion:

Order No. 57/2024 ensures that developers are held accountable for delivering the amenities they promise at the time of project registration. Non-compliance can result in penalties, protecting homebuyers and ensuring transparency in real estate transactions.

XXVI. Only Association of Allottees Can File a Complaint for Common Areas in a Completed Project

Case No.: Appeal No. CC00500000054098

Citation: Swapnil Anandrao Patil & Rajnand Dinkar Satpute Vs Vertical Infra

Coram: Shri Ajoy Mehta, Chairperson Maha RERA

Order Date: 2022-05-10

Section: Section 31

Background:

This case involved Swapnil Anandrao Patil and Rajnand Dinkar Satpute, both homebuyers in a completed project by Vertical Infra. The issue concerned whether an individual could file a complaint related to common areas in a project that had already been marked as completed.

Facts of the Case:

- Swapnil Patil and Rajnand Satpute, homebuyers in the Vertical Infra project, filed a complaint regarding the incomplete or defective common areas in the project, despite it being declared complete by the developer.
- The developer, Vertical Infra, argued that the complaint could not be filed by individuals and that such grievances regarding common areas should be submitted by the association of allottees or the housing society, particularly after the project was declared complete.
- The issue was brought before the MahaRERA Authority to clarify who had the standing to file such complaints under the RERA framework.

Respondent-Developer's Argument:

- Vertical Infra asserted that post-completion, individual homeowners lose the right to raise issues concerning common areas. Instead, only the association of allottees or a recognized housing society could file complaints related to deficiencies in common areas.
- They further argued that accepting individual complaints for common areas after project completion could result in fragmented and inconsistent claims, causing complications in the redressal process.

Key Legal Issues:

1. Authority to File Complaints: Whether individual allottees can file complaints concerning common areas in a completed project, or if only the association of allottees has this right.
2. Post-Completion Grievances: The scope of RERA's protection in addressing common area grievances once the project is officially declared complete.

RERA's Ruling:

- Only Association Can File Complaints: RERA ruled that once the project is marked as completed and possession is handed over, only the association of allottees or a registered housing society can file a complaint concerning the common areas of the project. Individual homebuyers do not have the right to file such complaints after the project's completion.
- Collective Redressal for Common Areas: The ruling emphasized that all residents share common areas, and as such, grievances should be raised collectively by the association, ensuring a unified approach to the management and resolution of issues related to these spaces.

Conclusion:

In the case of Swapnil Anandrao Patil & Rajnand Dinkar Satpute vs. Vertical Infra, the court clarified that individual allottees cannot file complaints concerning common areas in a completed project. This right is reserved for the association of allottees or the housing society, ensuring that issues in common areas are addressed collectively.

XXVII. Can Maha RERA Deregister a Project on the Promoter's Request?

Case No.: Regulatory Case No. 01 of 2022

Citation: Turf Estate Joint Venture LLP - Applicant-Promoter, Kesari Realty Venture LLP & Others - Respondents

Coram: Shri Ajoy Mehta, Hon'ble Chairperson MahaRERA

Order Date: 2022-09-02

Section: Section 3

Background:

This case involved Turf Estate Joint Venture LLP as the applicant-promoter, along with Kesari Realty Venture LLP and other respondents. The core issue was whether MahaRERA could deregister a real estate project at the request of the promoter. The case also questioned whether project registration is eternal or can be relinquished and what remedies are available to the respondents (allottees) when a promoter seeks deregistration without completing the project.

Facts of the Case:

- Turf Estate Joint Venture LLP sought deregistration of their real estate project from MahaRERA, claiming that the project was no longer viable and could not proceed in its current form.
- Approximately 22 out of 27 allottees had accepted refunds with interest and opted to exit the project, indicating their agreement with the promoter's decision to abandon the project.
- However, 5 respondents (allottees) refused the refund and opposed the deregistration, insisting that the project should be completed.
- The applicants argued that, under the RERA Act, the promoter holds the privilege of seeking project registration and extension,

and similarly, has the right to request deregistration when the project can no longer continue.

Promoter's Argument:

- The promoter contended that the project had become non-viable, and 2/3rd of the allottees had already opted to exit the project by accepting refunds with interest.
- The promoter argued that registration, which was granted under Section 5 of the RERA Act, was not meant to last in perpetuity. Since the purpose of registration had ceased due to the project's inability to proceed, it should be cancelled.
- Furthermore, they claimed that the RERA Act vests only the promoter with the privilege of seeking registration and extension, and this privilege extends to seeking deregistration when needed.

Key Legal Issues:

1. Authority to Deregister a Project: Whether Maha RERA has the authority to deregister a real estate project at the request of the promoter.
2. Duration of Project Registration: Whether the registration of a project granted by Maha RERA is intended to last indefinitely or can be revoked upon the promoter's request.
3. Remedies for Allottees: What recourse is available to allottees who refuse to accept the promoter's decision to abandon the project, despite part consideration being paid.

Maha RERA's Ruling:

- Deregistration is Permissible on Promoter's Request: Maha RERA ruled that it has the authority to deregister a project based on the promoter's request under certain conditions. Registration is not eternal, and once the purpose for which it was granted ceases to exist, it becomes infructuous. In this case, 2/3rd of the allottees had opted to exit the project, thus reinforcing the promoter's argument that the project cannot proceed.

- Protection of Minority Allottees: The authority acknowledged the objections of the 5 remaining allottees who refused the refund. The promoter had deposited their refund amount with 9% interest in a fixed deposit, ensuring their protection. However, Maha RERA noted that these allottees had also filed complaints under Section 31 of the RERA Act, which had been disposed of. Additionally, they had challenged the termination of their allotments before the Bombay High Court. Maha RERA refrained from interfering further, given the pending adjudication before the High Court.
- Registration Not Meant for Eternity: Maha RERA clarified that the RERA Act grants the privilege of registration and its extension to the promoter, but this privilege does not imply that the registration must last indefinitely. Once the project is abandoned, continuing registration serves no purpose.

Conclusion:

In the case of Turf Estate Joint Venture LLP vs. Kesari Realty Venture LLP, Maha RERA concluded that the promoter can seek deregistration of a project when it is no longer viable. Registration under the RERA Act is not meant to last indefinitely, and once a project ceases to exist, registration becomes irrelevant. However, the rights of minority allottees are protected, and they may seek redressal through other legal channels. The project was deregistered, and the promoter was barred from further advertising, marketing, or creating third-party rights in the project.

XXVIII. Submitting a False/Invalid Commencement Certificate

Case No.: Suo Moto Case No. 206 of 2021

Citation: Sai Builders and Developers, Shivsagar Gurucharan Yadav

Coram: Shri Ajoy Mehta, Hon'ble Chairperson Maha RERA & Shri (Dr.) Vijay Satbir Singh, Member 1

Order Date: 2021-09-08

Section: Section 7

Background:

The case was initiated suo moto by Maha RERA concerning Sai Builders and Developers, where the issue revolved around the submission of a false or invalid commencement certificate (CC). The project's promoter, Shivsagar Gurucharan Yadav, was accused of obtaining an invalid CC and misrepresenting its validity to allottees while collecting bookings and money based on the misrepresentation.

Facts of the Case:

- Sai Builders and Developers submitted a commencement certificate (CC) for their project, which was later discovered to be invalid and not legitimately issued by the competent authority.
- The promoter continued to accept bookings and money from prospective buyers by misrepresenting the validity of the CC.
- The Kalyan-Dombivli Municipal Corporation (KDMC) confirmed that the CC was invalid, and its issuance did not follow legal procedures.
- Maha RERA took up the case to investigate the matter and determine the appropriate action against the promoter.

Promoter's Argument:

- The promoter did not dispute the invalidity of the CC during the proceedings but argued that the project's registration should not be revoked as some buyers had already invested in the project.
- The promoter sought to rectify the issue and continue with the project under the corrected procedures.

Key Legal Issues:

1. Powers under Section 7: Whether Maha RERA has the authority to revoke a project's registration when the promoter engages in unfair practices such as submitting an invalid CC and misrepresenting its validity to buyers.
2. Protection of Allottees: How to safeguard the interests of both existing and prospective allottees who were misled by the promoter's actions and prevent further engagement with the project under false pretences.

Maha RERA's Ruling:

- Revocation of Registration: Maha RERA ruled that under Section 7 of the RERA Act, it has the authority to revoke the registration of a project if the promoter is found to have indulged in unfair practices, such as submitting a false CC and misrepresenting its validity to allottees. In this case, the promoter's actions were deemed deceptive and a violation of the Act.
- Safeguarding Allottees: To protect the interests of both existing and prospective allottees, Maha RERA revoked the registration of the project (Maha RERA Project Registration No. P51700026614), preventing the promoter from continuing to collect bookings or engaging further with buyers under false pretences.
- Implementation of Statutory Measures: Maha RERA directed all relevant departments, including the Secretary (Urban Development) of the Government of Maharashtra and all local planning authorities, to ensure that statutory certificates are uploaded immediately upon issuance on their respective websites.

Additionally, any changes or modifications must be updated in real-time to prevent similar instances in the future.

- Restraining Orders: The promoter was prohibited from advertising, marketing, booking, selling, or offering any apartments or buildings for sale in the project.

Conclusion:

In the case of Sai Builders and Developers, Maha RERA invoked its powers under Section 7 to revoke the registration of the project due to the submission of a false commencement certificate. This action was taken to safeguard the interests of allottees and prevent further misrepresentation. The order also emphasized the importance of timely and accurate uploads of statutory certificates by planning authorities to ensure transparency in the real estate sector.

XXIX. Procedure for Transferring or Assigning Promoters' Rights to a Third Party

Case No.: Circular no. 24 B/ 2024

Order Date: 29/10/2024

Background:

Circular 24B of 2024 was issued to streamline the process for the transfer or assignment of a promoter's rights in a real estate project to a third party. It provides clarity on the requirements and procedures for such a transfer, aiming to address ambiguities from previous circulars (Circular 24 of 2019 and Circular 24A of 2021).

Key Points:

1. Eligibility and Approval:

- Only promoters with an active RERA registration and no pending compliance issues may apply for a transfer or assignment of their project rights to a third party.
- The transferring promoter must obtain prior written consent from at least two-thirds of the project's allottees, ensuring the decision respects the interest of majority stakeholders.
- Maha RERA approval is mandatory before finalizing any transfer, subject to verification of project compliance and outstanding obligations.

2. Requirements and Documentation:

- The promoter must submit an application to Maha RERA along with a detailed transfer proposal. This proposal must outline the reasons for transfer, details of the new promoter, and an assurance of continuity of project obligations.
- Financial transparency is essential, including full disclosure of project funds, payments, and an affidavit stating that all dues to allottees and authorities are settled.

- The incoming promoter must agree to comply with the original project terms, including timelines, quality standards, and customer commitments as per the registered agreement.

3. **Review Process by Maha RERA:**
   - Upon receiving the application, Maha RERA will conduct a thorough review to assess compliance with RERA regulations, past records of the transferring promoter, and the financial viability of the incoming promoter.
   - Maha RERA may impose additional conditions on the incoming promoter to ensure that all project obligations are honoured.

4. **Clarifications to Previous Circulars:**
   - Circular 24 of 2019: Defined the initial procedures for promoter rights transfers but lacked detailed compliance requirements. Circular 24B clarifies that these requirements must be fully met and that any unresolved dues must be settled before initiating the transfer.
   - Circular 24A of 2021: Added conditions for transparency in financial disclosures; Circular 24B reinforces these by mandating a more stringent financial review process and the full disclosure of all dues and project expenses.

Maha RERA's Directives:

- Maha RERA has mandated that the promoter rights transfer process be transparent and protect the interests of all stakeholders, including allottees, investors, and project employees.
- Promoters transferring rights are strictly prohibited from marketing or advertising the project under the new promoter until Maha RERA approval is obtained.
- Failure to comply with the conditions of Circular 24B may result in the suspension of the project registration, penalties, or other corrective actions as deemed necessary by Maha RERA.

Conclusion:

Circular 24B of 2024 introduces a structured process for transferring or assigning promoters' rights in a project, focusing on compliance, financial transparency, and stakeholder protection. By building on the guidelines set out in Circulars 24 of 2019 and 24A of 2021, Circular 24B ensures the continuity of project obligations and reinforces Maha RERA's commitment to accountability in real estate transactions.

XXX. Registration of Agreement for Sale/Sale Deed of Units in Excluded Real Estate Projects and Defining Completion of Plotted Projects

- **Order No.:** Order No. 62 of 2024
- **Date Issued:** 22/10/2024

Background:

Order No. 62 of 2024 addresses the registration requirements for agreements for sale and sale deeds in real estate projects excluded from RERA registration. It also provides a clear definition of what constitutes the completion of plotted real estate projects, responding to previous ambiguities and aligning with RERA's objective of safeguarding buyer interests.

Key Points:

1. Registration of Agreements and Sale Deeds in Exempted Projects:

- Real estate projects exempted from RERA registration, such as those with fewer than eight units or on land less than 500 square meters, have historically faced uncertainties regarding the registration of agreements for sale and sale deeds.
- The order mandates that, despite exemption from RERA registration, developers of these projects must still register agreements for sale and sale deeds to ensure transparency and protect the rights of allottees.
- The provision aims to prevent future disputes by clearly documenting the terms of sale, obligations, and rights, even if the project itself does not require RERA registration.

2. Defining Completion of Plotted Real Estate Projects:

- Order No. 62 specifies that a plotted real estate project is considered "complete" when all development activities, as per the sanctioned layout, are finished. This includes necessary infrastructure such as roads, utilities, drainage, and common amenities promised at the time of sale.

- The order highlights that completion is not limited to the mere sale of plots; rather, it depends on the actual availability of functional infrastructure and amenities as per approved plans.
- This definition ensures that buyers have clarity on project deliverables and prevents premature closure or handover of projects by developers without fulfilling all infrastructure commitments.

3. Applicability and Compliance:

- The order applies to all real estate promoters, irrespective of project size, to promote transparency and accountability in projects that were previously exempt.
- Developers must provide proof of infrastructure completion and utility installation to obtain a "completion certificate" for plotted projects. This certificate will serve as evidence of project completion under RERA guidelines.
- Non-compliance with these guidelines, especially in terms of registering agreements and completing promised infrastructure, may result in penalties or legal action from Maha RERA.

Maha RERA's Directives:

- Maha RERA requires that promoters of exempted projects register agreements and sale deeds for all units, ensuring that contractual terms and buyer rights are formalized even outside RERA's direct registration framework.
- Completion certificates for plotted projects must now only be issued after verifying that all necessary infrastructure is in place and fully operational.
- The directives reinforce the need for full accountability and adherence to sanctioned plans, ensuring that buyer interests are protected even in projects that fall outside RERA's primary registration scope.

Conclusion:

Order No. 62 of 2024 establishes mandatory registration for agreements and sale deeds in exempt real estate projects and clarifies the criteria for the completion of plotted projects. By standardizing documentation and completion standards, this order enhances transparency and protection for buyers, ensuring that developers adhere to their commitments in all types of real estate projects.

XXXI. Mandatory Disclosure of Brokerage or Commission in Sale Agreements

- **Order No.:** 15a of 2024
- **Date Issued:** 22/10/2024

Background

Maha RERA issued Order No. 15a of 2024 to address the lack of transparency regarding brokerage or commission payments to real estate agents in property transactions. This order ensures that all sale agreements between developers and purchasers, facilitated by registered real estate agents, explicitly disclose the amount of commission or brokerage, including taxes, payable to the agents.

The order aims to enhance accountability and clarity in transactions, protecting the interests of all parties involved, particularly buyers, by providing full transparency about financial obligations.

Key Points

1. Mandatory Disclosure of Commission or Brokerage

The order mandates that sale agreements facilitated by registered real estate agents must explicitly mention the commission or brokerage amount, including applicable taxes, payable to the agent.

The payment details should clearly specify, the party responsible for payment (developer, buyer, or both) and the total amount, inclusive of all applicable taxes.c This ensures that buyers and developers are fully aware of their financial responsibilities towards the agents, avoiding disputes or hidden costs.

2. Applicability

The order applies to all agreements for sale where a registered real estate agent is involved and transactions facilitated by agents in both registered and exempt real estate projects. The directive ensures uniformity in the documentation process across all Maha RERA-supervised transactions.

3. Impact on Developers, Buyers, and Agents

- For Developers: Ensures clarity in financial obligations related to brokerage payments, reducing disputes with buyers and agents.
- For Buyers: Provides transparency regarding additional costs beyond the property price, enabling informed decisions.
- For Agents: Strengthens their position by formalizing commission or brokerage terms in legal agreements, ensuring timely payments.

Conclusion

Order No. 15a of 2024 reinforces Maha RERA's commitment to transparency in real estate transactions by mandating the disclosure of brokerage or commission in sale agreements. By formalizing these payments, the order ensures fairness, accountability, and a clearer understanding of financial obligations, ultimately fostering trust among developers, buyers, and agents.

XXXII. Maha RERA Orders for Rectification of Structural Defects

Complaint Regarding Structural Defects in Pune Housing Project

- **Complaint No.:** CC005000000106546
- **Date of Order:** 11/11/2024

Background

The complaint was filed by Sharad Agrawal against the Pune Housing and Area Development Board (MHADA) regarding a registered project identified as "Const. 378 LIG, 331 MIG, 154 HIG T." The project, located in Haveli, Pune, bears MahaRERA Project Registration No. P52100009644.

The complainant sought MahaRERA's intervention to direct the promoter to rectify pending structural and infrastructural issues, including water seepage, incomplete fire safety measures, solar fittings, and inadequate water supply.

Key Points

1. Structural Defects Raised by the Complainant

The complainant reported persistent structural defects such as water seepage, improper door installations, and damaged plasterwork. Issues with the solar fittings, firefighting equipment, and water supply in the project were highlighted. Despite repeated communication with the MHADA officials between 2018 and 2021, the defects remained unresolved.

2. Developer's Non-Compliance

Although MHADA repaired some issues, such as leakage and plaster damage, it failed to rectify other reported defects, including incomplete solar fittings and water supply concerns. MHADA did not submit a comprehensive reply or upload the occupancy certificate (OC) on the MahaRERA portal despite obtaining the OC in 2018.

3. Maha RERA's Observations

The project was deemed complete on-site in 2018, as evidenced by Form 4 and the OC obtained from Pimpri Chinchwad Municipal Corporation. However, essential updates were not reflected on the Maha RERA platform. Under Section 14(3) of RERA, the promoter is obligated to rectify structural defects reported by allottees within five years of possession.

4. Compliance and Relief Measures

The complainant was directed to provide a detailed written notice to the promoter regarding unresolved defects within 30 days. MHADA was instructed to address and rectify these defects within a subsequent 30-day period. Failure to comply would entitle the complainant to seek compensation by filing a formal complaint under Sections 71 and 72 of RERA.

Maha RERA's Directives

- MHADA must rectify the structural and service-related defects as reported by the complainant within the stipulated timeframe.
- The promoter is required to ensure complete compliance with Section 14(3) of RERA and upload all necessary documentation, including the OC, to the MahaRERA portal.
- In case of non-compliance, the complainant is entitled to file a compensation claim before the Adjudicating Officer of MahaRERA.

Conclusion

The MahaRERA order underlines the promoter's responsibility to address structural defects within the defect liability period. By directing Pune Housing and Area Development Board to take corrective measures, Maha RERA aims to uphold buyer protection and ensure adherence to the Real Estate (Regulation and Development) Act, 2016.

Part 9

Best Practices under RERA across India

1. Maha RERA: Real-Time Project Tracking System

Maha RERA's digital dashboard offers real-time tracking of project progress, including financial and physical milestones, and is accessible to buyers and authorities.

A nationwide dashboard for real-time updates can ensure transparency and accountability.

2. Gujarat RERA: Early Warning System (EWS)

Gujarat RERA has implemented an EWS that flags projects showing early signs of distress, such as fund shortages or delays.

States should adopt an EWS to pre-emptively address project delays and prevent consumer losses.

3. Karnataka RERA: Buyer Voting Mechanism for Insolvent Projects

Allows buyers to collectively vote on the future of insolvent projects, such as appointing new developers or liquidating assets.

States lacking a structured approach for handling stalled projects can adopt this participatory decision-making process.

4. Tamil Nadu RERA: Integration with Local Planning Authorities

TNRERA collaborates closely with local urban development bodies to ensure quicker and seamless project approvals.

States should ensure such integration to reduce bureaucratic hurdles and expedite clearances.

5. Delhi RERA: AI-Powered Compliance Monitoring

Delhi RERA is exploring AI tools to automatically detect compliance failures, such as missed deadlines or irregular fund usage.

All states can implement AI for proactive monitoring and enforcement.

6. UP RERA: Stalled Projects Resolution Policy

UP RERA has a dedicated policy to revive stalled projects through developer-buyer mediation, third-party involvement, or financial restructuring.

Other states can adopt such structured frameworks to address the growing number of incomplete projects.

7. Rajasthan RERA: Land Title Certification

RERA in Rajasthan collaborates with revenue departments to ensure land title clarity before project approval.

A robust land title verification mechanism should be mandatory nationwide to prevent disputes.

8. Haryana RERA: Graded Penalty System

Haryana RERA uses a graded penalty system based on the severity of non-compliance, encouraging developers to rectify issues quickly.

Other states can adopt this fair approach to incentivize compliance.

9. Kerala RERA: Climate-Resilient Construction Guidelines

Kerala mandates projects to comply with climate-resilient construction practices, considering the state's vulnerability to floods and landslides.

States facing environmental challenges should implement region-specific construction guidelines.

10. Telangana RERA: Blockchain for Property Records

Telangana is piloting blockchain technology to maintain immutable and transparent property records linked to RERA projects.

Blockchain can be adopted nationwide for secure and fraud-proof property records.

11. Punjab RERA: Legal Aid Clinics

Punjab RERA offers free legal aid clinics to educate and assist buyers in filing complaints or understanding legal provisions.

Other states can establish such clinics to bridge the legal knowledge gap among homebuyers.

12. Goa RERA: Sustainable Development Certification

Goa RERA encourages developers to obtain green building certifications and rewards such projects with faster approvals.

Nationwide incentives for eco-friendly construction can promote sustainable real estate practices.

13. Madhya Pradesh RERA: Strict Penalties for Misleading Advertisements

MPRERA imposes hefty fines on developers for false or exaggerated marketing claims.

All states should strictly penalize misleading advertisements to protect consumers.

14. Odisha RERA: Digitization of Historical Records

Odisha is digitizing legacy real estate records to provide clarity on older projects under the Act.

Other states should digitize records for better accountability and historical data access.

15. Assam RERA: Focus on Regional Developers

Assam RERA conducts capacity-building programs for small and regional developers, helping them comply with RERA norms.

States with smaller developers can adopt this practice to bring inclusivity and ensure widespread compliance.

Recurring Practices and Their Benefits

1. RERA Conciliation Forums *(Maharashtra, Uttar Pradesh, Gujarat, Haryana, Karnataka, Madhya Pradesh, Bihar)*:

Promoters and allottees can resolve disputes amicably, reducing litigation costs and fostering trust.

2. QR Code Implementation *(Maharashtra, Uttar Pradesh, Kerala, Karnataka)*:

Project-specific QR codes enhance transparency by providing easy access to verified project details.

3. Circuit Courts *(Madhya Pradesh)*:

Mobile courts improve accessibility, particularly in remote regions, streamlining dispute resolution. Madhya Pradesh's authorities travel to Indore, Jabalpur, and Gwalior for hearings.

4. Real-Time Project Tracking *(Tamil Nadu, Gujarat, Maharashtra)*:

Digital platforms ensure up-to-date project information for buyers and authorities, increasing transparency and accountability.

5. Agent Training and Certification *(Maharashtra, Uttar Pradesh)*:

Professional development for real estate agents builds trust and reduces disputes during transactions.

6. Defect Liability *(Telangana)*:

Clear guidelines enforce promoter accountability for structural defects and ensure rectifications are made within specified timeframes.

7. Allottee Grievance Redressal Officer *(Maharashtra)*:

Dedicated officers improve customer satisfaction and expedite complaint resolution for project-related issues.

As we conclude this exploration of RERA and its transformative impact on the real estate landscape, it becomes evident that this legislation is more than just a regulatory framework—it is a beacon of accountability, transparency, and empowerment for all stakeholders. From ensuring timely project completions to fostering trust between developers and buyers, RERA exemplifies the potential of proactive governance. By examining innovative practices across states, we have seen how collaboration, technology, and forward-thinking policies can bridge gaps, resolve conflicts, and pave the way for a sustainable real estate ecosystem.

This journey underscores the importance of continuous evolution and adaptation in governance to address emerging challenges and opportunities. RERA is not just a legal mechanism but a paradigm shift, placing the consumer at the heart of the real estate industry. As stakeholders, our shared responsibility lies in upholding these principles, ensuring that the promise of RERA becomes a lived reality for generations to come. Let this book serve as both a guide and an inspiration to embrace the transformative power of transparency, fairness, and innovation in real estate.

www.ingramcontent.com/pod-product-compliance
Lightning Source LLC
LaVergne TN
LVHW091300150826
845673LV00006B/1483

* 9 7 9 8 8 9 6 7 3 3 7 8 2 *